Cyril 47-61

CHARITY MAIN

STUDIES IN
BRITISH LABOUR HISTORY
General Editor: Huw Beynon

CHARITY MAIN

A Coalfield Chronicle

by

Mark Benney

" . . . the rubbish heap at the collieries, where poor people grubbed among the stones, and picked up the fragments of coal accidentally mixed with them, was dubbed with the name of Charity Main."

R. L. GALLOWAY
Annals of Coal Mining

EP Publishing Limited
1978

First published by George Allen and Unwin Limited,
London, 1946

Republished 1978 by
EP Publishing Limited
East Ardsley, Wakefield
West Yorkshire, England

ISBN 0 7158 1343 9

British Library Cataloguing in Publication Data
Benney, Mark
    Charity Main. – (Studies in British labour history).
    1. Coal mines and mining – England –
    Durham (County) – History
    2. Coal mines and mining – England –
    Northumberland – History
    I. Title II. Series
    338.2'7' 209428   HD9551.7.D/
    ISBN 0–7158–1343–9

Please address all enquiries to EP Publishing Limited
(address as above)

Printed in Great Britain by
Redwood Burn Limited
Trowbridge & Esher

Foreword

I WOULD first call the attention of the reader to the sub-title of this book—A *Coalfield* Chronicle. Although the whole purpose of the book is to help the public to make up its mind about the future of the most vital of our industries, I should not like to leave anywhere the impression that the picture I have painted is generally true. The British coal industry divides itself naturally into twenty-five administrative regions, each with its own marked differences of character. Within a single region even, as I hope this book will make clear, the widest varieties of social and technical conditions can be found. I ask no more of my readers than that they shall accept this book as giving a true and fair account of a region producing about one-seventh of the annual coal output of the country.

Believing as I do that technical, economic and financial data have no meaning apart from the men and women whose activities they so wanly reflect, I had no choice but to present my observations in a human guise. I must make it clear, therefore, that all the persons, name-places and commercial undertakings described in this book are imaginary ones, built up out of bits and pieces of fact to avoid giving offence to any living individuals. I have tried to invent nothing that is not typical of a northern coalfield, nothing that would leave even the hastiest reader with a false impression.

MARK BENNEY.

June, 1945.

CONTENTS

Chapter One

THE VILLAGE

IF you travel ten miles up the crowded, carious mouth of the river—past the shipyards where a temporary wartime clangour overlays the slow rot of permanent depression, under the suspension bridges of the city, along past those gruesome slums with the highest tuberculosis rate of the country—you reach a point where the channel becomes too shallow for traffic, where the water is still quite clean and sparkling and salmon still survive. A dozen miles to the south of this point lies the mining village of East Tanthope.

In the early spring of 1944 a middle-aged temporary civil servant named Johnson got off a bus outside the East Tanthope Co-operative Society stores and, consulting a piece of paper in his hand, approached a group of men squatting on their heels at a nearby corner.

He asked them where he should find a certain street. They stared at him, and at each other, shaking their heads in a slow bewilderment.

" Who do 'ee want, hinny ? " someone asked.

" Sam Forgan," Johnson said.

A look of relief came over the faces of the squatting men. They vied with each other in giving instructions and information, saying that he was bound to find Sam in, that he had not long returned from the pit being on foreshift, and that like as not he would be sitting down to his tea at this moment. Johnson thanked the men and went off in the direction they had indicated. He was smiling, thinking of the curious tribal dignity these men achieved by their habit of squatting on one heel.

He found the house he was looking for in a narrow

unpaved row of two-storied cottages. A stranger in this part of the country, he had never seen anything quite so insulting to the eye before. He had never imagined that human dwellings could be built with such flaunting disregard for human values. Outside each cottage, dumped in the dirt road, were piles of coal. Two men, shovelling their piles into little sheds fronting the cottages, stopped to stare at him as he turned into the row.

A small, thin, excitable young man answered Johnson's knock. This was Sam Forgan. He greeted Johnson as an old friend, with so much hubbub that he seemed like a whole railway station full of people welcoming a whole trainload of kinsmen. He showered greetings, explanations, injunctions and welcomes almost simultaneously.

" Mak' yerself at hame, man—off wi' yer jacket noo, off wi' it, ye canna stand on ceremony in this hoose." He tugged at Johnson's jacket, moved papers from a chair, shooed away a thumb-sucking infant and introduced him to his wife, all in a matter of seconds. " Ah waited tea for 'ee, man—ye mun be starving. Hinny, is that tea ready ? " he asked his wife.

Mrs. Forgan was a pale, peaked, solemn-eyed, shy little woman who looked fifteen or so in spite of the thumb-sucking evidence to the contrary. She had laid out already on the table a mountainous high tea—pies and scones and plates of meat and jam. Johnson and the miner sat at the table in their shirt sleeves, grinning at each other across the piles of food. Mrs. Forgan did not sit with them. She busied herself frying chips at the stove, refilling cups, cutting bread and butter or pushing the infant away from her skirts.

" Man, the time we had in Lunnon—Ah'll nee forget it ! " Sam kept saying, breathlessly happy. A week before Johnson, on behalf of his Ministry, had escorted six miners with high output records on a visit to the Fuel Research Station in Greenwich. Sam had been among them, the youngest and most impressible.   Because Johnson was new to his job and was anxious to make contacts among the miners, and because Sam Forgan had been the only voluble member of a party that had been on the whole dour and undemonstrative, this friendship had developed between them.

Sam had never been to London before, and now, as he sat, eating his tea, the impressions crowded back, incoherently and incredibly.   " Man, that unnergroond ! Eeh, if t'pit wor like that Ah· wouldna mind hewing coals. . . . Mind 'ee, Ah'd niver find ma way aroond that plaace, Ah wouldna !   Aye, an' yer flat—Ah wor telling the wife aboot yer flat, but she divvent believe it . . . ten floors up, wi' a lift an' porters an' things !   Man, t'wor like ye see in pictures. . . ."

" Eeh, man, Ah've heard nowt but Lunnon, Lunnon, Lunnon since ye've bin back," Mrs. Forgan said to Johnson placidly.   " Ah hope he didna misbehave hissel'—he gets awfu' bad sometimes when he's had a pint."

" A' whee, hinny, Ah didna, Ah tell ye ! " Sam appealed anxiously to Johnson for confirmation.   " Ah didna do any wrang, did Ah noo ? "

" Sam set an example for us all," Johnson assured the wife.   " But how about the Research Station, Sam ?   What did you think of that ? "

This, after all, had been the real point of the London visit : that these miners should see with their own eyes what a prodigious part coal played in the scientific scheme of things.   The intricate minuscule world of the hydrocarbons had been laid open for their inspection.   They had watched the shining black stuff they spent their lives extracting from the treacherous earth passing through crazy erections of glass tubes and steel chambers to emerge in a hundred unfamiliar forms—white powders, pink liquids, yellow pastes, brown gases.   What had it all meant to them, Johnson wondered ?

" Eeh, t'wor heavy stuff, that," Sam said. " Ah couldna mak' head nor tail o' maist. Mind 'ee, t'wor inter-resting. That petrol-stuff—aye, t'wor like sponge, hinny, solid sponge, an' when ye squeezed it, why, it went awhee like ordinary petrol ! An' t'flames, aye, they flames'll gie the Nazis summat t'think aboot ! But Ah couldna unnerstan' maist o't. Ah'm nie scholard."

" Aye, he's nie scholard, is Sam," his wife echoed.

" Mind 'ee," Sam said quickly, anxious not to be mis-understood, " Ah like a bit read noo an' then, stories like, 'tis only that Ah canna ha'e patience wi' the heavy stuff."

The little room was clean as a new pin, with cheerfully papered walls, but everything in it was rather too big. The fire in the polished cooking range, the table, the armchair, the sideboard. You had to squeeze round the furnishings to move from one side of the room to the other. There was a room beyond which Johnson had assumed to be a parlour ; but when he caught a glimpse through the door he saw it was furnished as a bedroom.

" Have you only got two rooms here, Sam ? " Johnson asked in surprise when he noticed this.

" Aye," Sam said, " two rooms an' t'scullery. They's two more upstairs, but they divvent belang t'us. Auld Tom Kelso's daughter has her bit furniture up there, till her man comes back from th'army, but she divvent live here."

" An' reet glad Ah am, too," Mrs. Forgan said firmly. " Ah dinna want bairns squawking ower ma head aal dee lang, Ah'll tell ye."

" Awhee, hinny, it's no' t'bairns Ah'm scared aboot, it's their fairthers," Sam said meaningly.

After tea, Sam spent five minutes in the bedroom with his wife. They had pushed the door to, but Johnson could hear everything they said. Sam was trying to persuade her to lend him five shillings. It seemed he had spent all his pocket-money on the trip to London, and had been borrowing from her ever since.

" Ah'll gie it thee this once," she said finally, " but mind, tha'll hae ter work t'Sunday shift this week ! "

" Ah will, hinny, Ah will," he assured her, and there was a chink as he pocketed the coins. When he emerged from the bedroom he took his jacket off the back of a chair and turned to Johnson with a broad grin. " A'whee, man, we'll gan awhee ower t'Club."

Leaving Mrs. Forgan to the housework, the two men left the house and threaded their way through a maze of allotments to the Workmen's Club. As they approached Sam Forgan pointed out the new two-storied, stucco-fronted building set about with shrubbery, dilating proudly on the contrast it offered to the surrounding building standards. It had been erected just before the war at a cost of two thousand pounds, he said—and had already paid for itself. Nobody made a profit out of it, not even the brewers, for the beer sold was co-operative beer. There were free concerts every week, a free lending library, and lectures and classes in the winter. Two or three times a year every member received a voucher entitling him to a pint of free beer. Women were only allowed in the club for the week-end concerts. Obviously Sam Forgan thought there was no other club in the world like it.

On a notice board in the entrance hall he pointed proudly to an accountant's statement, which showed that an average of five hundred pounds a week was taken over the bar.

They went into a long bleak bar-room where a hundred or so men were sitting round tables with pint pots before them. Sam, who had taken on the air of a showman, seemed vaguely ashamed of the number of vacant places at the tables.

" It's Thursday neet—ye dinna get many wi' pocket-money left by Thursday," he said apologetically.

As they made their way towards the further end of the room heads turned slowly to watch the progress of the stranger in their midst. Sam stopped before a table where a group of silent men were sitting. He introduced Johnson.

" Yere's the man from the Ministry Ah wor tellin' ye of," he said.

They all shook hands with a minimum of words, and chairs were found for the two newcomers. Five pairs of steady eyes studied Johnson. " Will ye have a pint ? " someone asked.

By contrast with his friends Sam was almost hysterically voluble. This was the Chairman of the Lodge, he told Johnson, and this was the Secretary. And this was old Tom Kelso, the assistant checkweighman, whose daughter had the rooms upstairs. " He wants ta knaw what we think of t'pit," Sam told them to explain Johnson's presence.

In the course of an hour and three pints of beer their opinion emerged unmistakably. Tanthope Colliery was the worst in the county. The manager was a bully. The agent thought only of cutting prices. They were working only the thinnest seams now and saving the best coal for after the war. The underground conditions were a scandal. The travelling was too long and the roadways too low. The owners were economising on equipment and endangering the lives of the men.

All this was told to Johnson with a wealth of intimate detail and endless illustrative stories. Johnson, anxious to prove himself a sympathetic listener, asked only sufficient questions to keep the talk going ; indeed he was not equipped to probe behind what he felt were often conventional complaints made simply because he was a sympathetic outsider. For although Johnson had read a good deal about the industry, he had not been in the region long enough to pick up the meaning of local technical terms, and he had yet to go down a pit. More than once he felt certain, however, that these men were distorting the facts about the local pit, painting in unnecessarily sombre colours, in order to fit their situation into the traditional 'Miner's Case.' His conviction grew when one of the men uttered passionate protests against the royalty system.

"Why should we pay eightpence a ton to some pot-bellied landowner just because he owns the surface under which the coal lies ?"

"But you don't," Johnson said in surprise. "The coal royalties have been nationalised. Royalties are paid to the Coal Commission now."

They did not appear to have heard of that, and were unwilling to believe him until he had given them all the facts about the 1938 White Paper and the working of the Coal Commission. It was evident that miners, like other people, are reluctant to abandon a good grievance simply because the occasion for it has passed.

During the course of this hour, only one of the five men had maintained throughout the same impassive silence of the first few minutes. This was the old man, Tom Kelso. A small man in his seventies, with a long red face and completely bald head, he was dressed in a shiny blue serge suit with a thick silver chain dangling across his waistcoat. He smoked a clay pipe with a tin lid on it, and sat upright with enormous bony hands on his knees. At no time did he utter a single word of his own volition. Only when a question was directed unmistakably at him would he slowly remove his pipe from his mouth, moisten his lips, and utter a monosyllabic 'aye' or 'nay' as the case might be. But his eyes darting round the table from speaker to speaker revealed an alert and intelligent mind. The old man still worked underground, and near the coal face, although he was given light tasks.

Sam, affected by his fourth pint, was becoming talkative enough for two. In London, in his cups, he had shown an irrepressible tendency to recite a dramatic monologue about a crippled boy on a mountainside. To-night he insisted on telling, with unnecessary drama; exactly how he came to lose the index finger of his right hand in a pit accident.

There was no escaping a single detail of the story. Waving the mutilated member before Johnson's eyes, he described how a deputy came into the place where he and his ' marrow ' were working, and had refused to fire a shot.

" Ask anyone," he challenged Johnson. " Arthur Riskin, it wor. ' Ye canna get nee shots fired here,' he said. Divvent that mean the plaace worn't safe ta wark in ? " He stared at Tom Kelso. " Divvent it, Tom ? "

Tom Kelso nodded.

While his friend was setting timber, Sam went on, he had started to hew the coal. A large lump had fallen from the face and knocked out a nearby prop. As he told the story, Sam's face became tense with the effort to convey exactly, so that Johnson could share it with him, the special quality of terror of that moment when his small dark cramped world caved in around him. " Crash ! " he shouted excitedly, " Crash ! Ma lamp wor buried, see ? Aal Ah could hear wor a sort o' thunder ! "

" Crash, bang ! " he said lamely.

The others had obviously heard the story several times before, but they were not bored. The union officials, however, seemed to think Sam was laying stress on the wrong points. Particularly the Lodge Secretary seemed to think so. Not the injury itself, but the inadequate compensation paid for it, was the thing to impress on the man from the Ministry.

" Aaight weeks ainly ! Thirty-five bob a week—an' him wi' a wife an' bairn ! " he repeated at intervals.

Then Johnson noticed that the old man Tom Kelso had two fingers missing from his right hand. " Was that also a pit accident ? " he asked. Slowly the old man raised his hand and looked at it, almost fondly. Then he removed the clay pipe from his mouth.

" Aye," he said.

Perhaps it was the four pints of beer, but suddenly there came upon Johnson an obscure but powerful sense of privilege, of wondrous good fortune in simply being allowed to sit with these men in their own club and speak with them. He laid an imploring hand on the old man's knee and spoke hurriedly.

" Sam tells me that your daughter has a couple of furnished rooms that she doesn't use. I'd like to live in this village. Do you think your daughter might let her rooms to me ? "

Tom Kelso stared at him, his pipe halfway to his mouth. He seemed to consider the idea for an interminable time before he spoke.

" Aye," he said at last. " She might."

So two days later Johnson brought his bags from the hotel where he had been staying in the city, and took possession of his new quarters. A most convenient arrangement had been arrived at, whereby the rooms would be cleaned for him and a fire laid daily, and he would have an evening meal with the Kelso family.

Yet after his first evening alone in those two rooms he was almost on the point of moving out again from a sheer sense of intrusion, of having loutishly invaded the most private recesses of a simple young woman's heart. The two rooms as he found them had never been lived in, although all the smallest appurtenances of living were there ready, even down to the tablet of soap in the soapdish on the washstand in the bedroom. They were a home that a young wife had fashioned for a life that was yet to begin. Every stick of furniture, every stitch of linen, every ornament and pot and pan was new with a quite startling newness. It had all been bought, piece by piece, with infinite care and sacrifice and the most appalling bad taste, at the great Co-operative Society store in the city ; lovingly and patiently brought together to give body to a fumed-oak dream of home. Never, surely, was so genteel a vision imposed so incongruously on its surroundings. The cottage, the village, the slagheap behind the village, all insisted on a harsh raw elemental scheme of life, where the cardinal virtues might flourish but refinements and comforts were never intended to have place. And here was a bedroom suite of degenerate 'modernistic' design, and a china cabinet containing a twenty-one piece tea set coloured black with silver spots, and framed mirrors on the wall, and a revolving bookcase, and satin runners on the sideboard and table, and a cubistic hearthrug : the appointments of two young people who when courting had twice a week boarded a luxury coach and gone to the cinema in the city, who from newspaper and radio had gathered ill-defined images and desires at variance with the slagheap, and had symbolised their experience with the aid of a hire-purchase account. Among these varnished braveries Johnson moved gingerly, lest by breaking an ornament he shattered a dream.

Johnson had other cause to tread gingerly, too. He had expected the excitable Sam Forgan to welcome him as a neighbour. But to his surprise the young miner became ill at ease and almost surly with him. At first he was at a loss to explain this, but after a few days he realised that Sam was consumed with jealousy. He suspected that Johnson had arranged to rent the rooms just to be near his absurdly young-looking wife. He writhed visibly at the thought that, while he was absent at work, Johnson and his wife were alone under one roof. He was constantly dropping little hints about his preoccupation.

" Ah allus mak' Jeannie lock t'bedroom door when Ah'm gannin' on foreshift."

" Ah'd nee rest till Ah'd killt t'man that interfered wi' ma wife."

" 'Tis easy for an eddicated man ter mak' a fool o' a woman, but he canna mak' a fool o' a man so easy ! "

Johnson tried with a few white lies about himself to set

the poor man's mind at rest. For the most part he relied on spending as little time as possible in his rooms. He slept there, but more and more, when he had free time in the evenings, he spent it with the Kelso family.

The Kelsos lived in a colliery-owned house on the other side of the village, at the end of a long grey street lined on both sides with houses exactly similar. These houses were much larger than the privately-built cottage that Johnson now lived in, but, like that, had just two rooms on each floor. The street was geometrically straight and in a direct line with a colliery a mile across the fields at the end of it, and the prevailing wind blew steady streams of fine ash along it, straight off the slagheap. This made the nightly walk up the street a torture for Johnson, with his weak, bookish eyes ; but once in the house, where Mrs. Kelso was waiting with the water already boiling for his tea, he would have again that sense of wondrous good fortune and privilege.

Old Tom was not often in when Johnson arrived home from work, for he spent as much of his spare time as possible in the Club. But in the house, in any case, not he but his wife was the important person. She was about twice the size of her husband, an old lady of ample curves, never seen without a flowered apron. She had a large, fresh, gentle face with thin white hair drawn back over her ears, and a slow gentle smile that sometimes faded but never wholly disappeared.

Mrs. Kelso was constantly at work, baking bread and tarts and pasties, washing, mending, scouring, and above all serving an endless succession of meals—for, counting Johnson, she had seven mouths to feed, and no one seemed to eat at the same time as anyone else. Sometimes, when she had just finished one chore and before taking up another, she would sit on the edge of a chair for a moment.

" Eeh, but Ah'm tired ! " she would say, then laugh at herself. Her soft leather shoes, with bunions swelling out in unexpected places, would be pressed together, still for a while, under her chair. Then she would be up again, doing things in the scullery.

She worked so hard that Johnson, who had been brought up to regard anyone over sixty as infirm, was sometimes frightened for her. On Mondays, particularly, she and her daughter Mary would spend the entire day over the wash-tub, scrubbing the linen of seven people. Then came the spring-cleaning, when she not only scrubbed the house from top to bottom, but whitewashed the scullery and papered the living-room walls as well. At first he offered to help, but the thought of a man doing housework of any sort was considered by these women as being too ludicrous to be entertained.

Mrs. Kelso was garrulous in a soft, slow way, prepared to talk endlessly about her family. Indeed there was little else she could talk about, for apart from a morning's shopping in the city once or twice a year, and perhaps on an exceptionally fine summer's day a trip to the coast with the children, she never stirred outside the village. There was a time, she told Johnson, when she and Tom had used to take little jaunts together. But these gave her no pleasure, indeed usually ended in a quarrel, because Tom would always be wanting to call in for a drink somewhere, while she—well, never in her whole life had a drop of alcohol, not even port, passed her lips ! But that was thirty years ago. Now she would avoid even the walk down the street to the Co-op. stores if she could, because that necessitated taking off her apron and putting on her best coat and uncomfortable shoes : the children did not like to see her looking untidy out of doors. These were the things she would tell Johnson when he asked her why she went out so seldom. But occasionally he caught a hint of a deeper reason, of which she was not herself perhaps fully aware. Four of her men-folk were working at the pit, and at any moment of the day or night someone might come to the door to announce an accident. She would not have wished to be away from home if that moment ever came.

There were three sons, all married and with homes of their own, although Norman, the youngest, still had meals with the family occasionally because his wife worked night shift at the colliery canteen. All three were, like their father, silent, heavy-drinking men, who when they were not at the Club squatted with the other men at the corner-end.

Of the four daughters, only one was married to a miner ; she already had a large family of her own, so that Johnson saw little of her. There were three still at home. Mary, eldest of these, was Johnson's ' landlord,' a dark, slender, quiet woman with a young baby to preoccupy her. Sometimes when her father or one of her brothers came in drunk, her eyes would flash contemptuously, and Johnson would catch a glimpse of the fiercely genteel spirit that had gone to the making of that strange little home which he rented from her. The other two daughters were unmarried, although Connie, next in the scale of age, spent alternate evenings writing long letters to a young man in the forces and embroidering pillow-slips for her bottom drawer. Connie worked in a factory in the city, and suffered from toothaches, which gave her a dark passionate look beneath her mop of ginger hair.

Beryl, the ' baby ' of the household, was a short, buxom, very pretty girl of nineteen with a charming smile and manner, but so lazy that she would not even pour a cup of tea for herself if she could get someone else to do it for her. She too worked in the city, and spent most of her evenings there : two regular dances a week, two regular cinema jaunts, and anything else that came along. If she had to stay indoors for a half-hour in the evening, while waiting for a friend, she would switch on the radio and sing with the band : she learned the words of every new dance-tune within a few days of its first performance. On Sunday afternoon she taught infants in the village Sunday school.

Beryl did not appear to have any regular boy friend, although Johnson soon learned that appearances in these matters was very unreliable. It seemed to be the custom in these parts for a girl never to admit she was walking out with a boy until the matter became too obvious to conceal any longer. Finding out who your sister's fellow might be was a passionately favourite sport among the brothers of the locality. Mrs. Kelso once told Johnson that her son Norman, when he first began to suspect that Mary was walking out regularly with the boy she later married, followed her around for two whole evenings in order to confirm the exciting theory.

To Johnson, raised in a small family, the outstanding characteristic of the Kelsos was their quietness. They could sit around for hours together without seeming to exchange a single word. Old Mrs. Kelso might murmur away in the background, but none of the family bothered to listen. Only Beryl's passion for jazz introduced an occasional note of uproar into the household. No greetings were exchanged when someone left or entered the house. The girls, when they returned from work in the evening, received no more acknowledgement than a casual lift or turn of the head : and they themselves would sit straight down to their teas, already laid out, with an air of never having really left the house. The habits and preoccupations of each were so well known that communication was almost unnecessary. Tom and Mrs. Kelso never talked to each other. Even Mary's baby was an extraordinarily quiet baby, or at least any show of noise on its part was met with alarm and prompt if curious action. A cry, and the old lady would look agitated. A second cry, and she would go to a cupboard, produce a bottle, and pour out a spoonful of its contents to give to the baby. Almost invariably the baby would cease to cry. It was a few weeks before Johnson discovered what was in that sedative bottle. It was whisky. In reply to his polite but anguished protests, Mrs. Kelso said firmly that she had raised seven children with the aid of whisky, and they were all hale. There was nothing more to say.

It was a prosperous little household : with the money that he paid for his board and lodging, Johnson estimated the family income to total twelve pounds a week, of which less than a pound a week was spent on rent for two establishments and fuel. But it was a wartime prosperity, and the long-standing habits of the home were founded on poverty. He noticed this particularly with regard to food. The quantities of food made available at mealtimes were enormous : at the afternoon meal on Sundays, for instance, a large plate piled high with tight-packed meat and vegetables would be placed before him, of which, with the best will in the world, he could not eat a fourth part. But the food was all of the poorest quality—the cheapest meat, the cheapest vegetables, the cheapest jams, the cheapest fish, eked out with masses of home-baked pastry. Once he met Mary in the city on a shopping expedition, and volunteered to carry her heavy bag. The greengrocer's shop into which he followed her was stocked with the new season's first fruits, high-priced but certainly within range of the family income : new green peas, artichokes, lettuce, asparagus, new potatoes. But Mary paid no attention to these, and plunged into the darkest recesses of the shop where only the stodgiest and solidest vegetables were displayed, and here she filled a second shopping bag from among the lowest priced things available. Johnson, reared among the food-and-wine fetishes of the middle classes, could understand the necessity for such a choice when shopping for a large family on a limited budget ; what he could not understand was that there should be no reluctant loitering at the choicer counters, not even a hint of interest, before making such dull purchases.

The feeding habits of the Kelso family provided Johnson with material for much reflection. A cultivated interest in food requires the stimulus of social display and competition. But this stimulus, he was beginning to realise, was almost completely absent in a mining village. In that long grey street where the Kelsos lived, every family knew the essential facts about every other family's life. The peculiar economic organisation of the pits made this inevitable. Every Wednesday evening Tom Kelso, as assistant checkweighman of the miners' Lodge, made up the pit 'averages.' This was a record, for union purposes, of the production of every coalface in the pit and of the earnings of every man engaged on those faces. The income of every mining family, in so far as it was derived from the mine, was known to everybody. The pretensions of urban living were impossible here. No family could assume higher standards than its income warranted without incurring ridicule. Here, perhaps, part of the reason why miners made their demands on life as a community, not as individuals.

Another aspect of the village to which Johnson found it rather difficult to adjust himself was the almost complete segregation of the social life of the two sexes. All but the youngest women in the village left their own firesides only to go to another woman's. If they went to a cinema or music-hall, it was with daughters or neighbouring wives— seldom indeed with their husbands. The miners spent their free evenings in the Club or in the billiard room or bowling-green of the Welfare Institute. These were the two chief social institutions of the village, and access to them by the wives of the community was severely circumscribed.

Thus Johnson found that if he wanted to spend an evening with any of the pitmen, a good deal of beer drinking was necessary. Simple incapacity for drinking on the heroic scale of these men threw him into the company of the womenfolk on most evenings of the week, but always, on Sunday evenings, he made a point of being in old Tom Kelso's company.

For on Sunday evenings Tom left the village and went to drink whisky in the city. At five o'clock he would get up from his afternoon nap, have tea, brush his jacket very carefully, and take out the great silver watch and chain from the drawer it was always kept in while he was at home or at work. When the chain was arranged to his satisfaction he would put on his best cap. This process took at least a quarter of an hour to complete, for Tom's bones were stiff after sixty years of working in the pit, and no movement came to him easily. But when he was ready, and not before, he would look over to Johnson, who was waiting for this moment.

" Are ye gannin' wi' us t'toon to-neet, Frank ? " he would ask. And Johnson, who never dared take it for granted that his company was desired by the old man, would grin out his relief.

" If I may, Tom," he would say happily, and jump up.

In the bus together Johnson would ask all the mining questions he had been saving for this ride, and the old man would answer, monosyllabically if possible. But there were three points on the road where Tom would himself volunteer information, always, even after they had made the journey a dozen times together, the same. One was to point out the spot where a German bomber had been forced down in the early days of the war. Another was to point out a little valley where open-air mass meetings had been held in the 1840 strikes. The third, as they approached the city, was to indicate a derelict pit where he himself had worked as a boy.

" They's still good coal there," he would say judiciously, " if tha knaws where t'look for't."

In the city they visited the same places in the same order every week. In the first pub they had two whiskies apiece, which the barmaid had put aside for Tom ; that pub was right opposite the bus station. The Labour Club, their real objective, was a mile away on the other side of the city, but there were two more pubs on the way to relieve the tedium of the sombre masses of calcified capital lining the city streets. It was usually eight o'clock before they reached the club, and they would sit there for an hour drinking steadily and saying little. Then the itinerary was repeated in reverse, so that they reached the bus station just in time for the last bus. On the return journey there would be no conversation at all, for Tom became more silent than ever when drunk, while Johnson, brooding over his stomach linings, would contrive to stand as near to the platform as possible.

They would reach the village only a few minutes after the Club had turned out for the night. On all the corners in the neighbourhood of the premises groups of men would be standing with their arms round each other's shoulders, singing. This was the moment that Johnson really loved. For now old Tom would march unsteadily to the nearest group, break into it, and, with his arm round Johnson's shoulder, join solemnly in the chorus.

Chapter Two

THE PIT

THERE were nearly two hundred coal mines in the area administered from the regional offices where Johnson worked. By far the most intimate source of information about any individual colliery, readily available to a Ministry official, was the minutes of the pit production committees, which were sent in to the regional offices after each meeting. Johnson read the minutes relating to Tanthope colliery with particular care.

These committees were statutory bodies, giving equal

representation to management and men ; a payment of
three shillings for each meeting was made by the Ministry
to every member.   The primary function of the committees
was to discuss the production problems of the pit and
evolve solutions.   In the event of disagreement on any
issue the matter could be referred to the Regional Controller
for arbitration.   The pit production committee was the
obvious channel of enquiry for any miner who had
complaints to make concerning the working of the pits.

Much to Johnson's surprise he found that few indeed of
the grievances nightly aired in the East Tanthope Workmen's Club ever found their way into the minutes he read
at his office.   Indeed these minutes were so scanty that it
seemed nothing at all was discussed at the committee
meetings except the allocation of extra clothing coupons.
Occasionally there would be a complaint about inadequate
pneumatic pressure at the coal faces, or a unanimous opinion
would be recorded that the trainees being sent to the pit
were useless, or the management would warn the committee
about increasing absenteeism.   The union men on the
committee seemed quite unable to use its facilities for the
purpose intended.

Johnson raised this question quite early in his
acquaintance with the men in the club.   He tackled first
the Lodge officials, who were all members of the production
committee.

" How was it you didn't raise that matter about hewers
working in the hitches at the production committee last
week ? "

" A'whee, man, they dinna tak' notice o' yer there," they
told him.

" In that case, send a minority statement into the Ministry,
and we'll send someone down to investigate."

" Investigate ! " they said contemptuously, and would say
no more.   The same sort of attitude was revealed on another
occasion, when the Lodge secretary was complaining about

new faces being opened in the thinnest and least accessible seam in the pit.

" But you had a chance to stop that before the faces were started—you should have informed the Ministry," Johnson said.

They laughed at him. " We dinna knaw what they're doin' till it's done," they told him.

" But don't they discuss new development plans with you at the production committee ? " Johnson asked in amazement. " Of course not," they chorused.

" But you can insist on it—it's one of the statutory functions of the committee. That's what you get paid for ! "

" Insist ! " " Insist ! " Once again they laughed the subject contemptuously away.

It was clear that, for some reason or other, these men did not wish to use the facilities of the committee to anything like the limit of its constitution. Johnson saw a danger in that, and tried earnestly to point it out.

" Look," he said, " these committees were set up at the request of your own unions. You've clamoured for them for years. If you don't use them to the full now you've got them, you'll find they'll be used against you."

But though they were prepared to agree to any statement prophesying disaster for miners in the future, they were not prepared to change their attitude to the production committee. At first Johnson thought it was simply that the men had been unfortunate in their choice of representatives ; but he discovered that these same union officials could be very forthright and aggressive on wage-negotiating committees and deputations. No, it was not that. In part it was that to use the committee efficiently it was necessary to use the Ministry—and the miners distrusted the Ministry, not for the perhaps valid reason that it took more notice of the coalowners than of them, but because it was novel and had not yet become integrated into their traditional scheme of things.   But also it was in part something that Johnson, with his left-wing sympathies, dared hardly admit to himself.

Two or three little incidents had happened which startled him at the time of their occurrence, and added up into something rather ugly.   There was the case of the man with nystagmus, for instance.   A hardy little man with wildly flickering eyes and slow, inarticulate wits, he used to sit at a neighbouring table in the Club to the one the Lodge officials habitually sat at.   He was pointed out to Johnson as the latest victim of a long standing abuse imposed on the men by the colliery company.   The company owned two adjacent pits, some of the workings of which interconnected.   The common labour pool was drawn upon for both pits, and according to his luck in the quarterly cavilling (or allocation of working-places by lot), a man might find himself working in one pit for three months and in the other for the three months following.   In one pit only the Davy-type of oil safety lamp was used.   In the other pit electric caplamps were issued.   Because of this, Johnson was told, the incidence of eye diseases such as nystagmus was extremely high among the men, since the two types of lamps gave different intensities of light and the miner's eyes never had a chance to accustom themselves to one or the other.   The men demanded electric caplamps in both pits, and the owners' refusal to comply with this demand was responsible, it was said, for unnecessary suffering.

The issue, as it was presented to him, seemed to Johnson to be clearly one for Ministry investigation, and he got the case looked into.   The report that came back to him, checked and re-checked beyond question, gave a very different story.   Davy lamps were used in the one pit for the very good reason that the safety regulations forbade the use of any other type in a pit with those particular working conditions.   The incidence of nystagmus among the workers was no higher than the national incidence. The men had been offered Davy lamps in both pits, and had refused the offer. They had been offered a segregation of the cavils of the two pits, so that the same men would always work in the same pit; they had refused that too. They wanted only their own solution—electric caplamps in both pits. And the reason underlying this obstinacy was· that the safety regulations required that, where cap-lamps were used, one extra Davy lamp must be carried for every four of the electric type. By agreement, the men who carried the extra lamps were paid sixpence a shift. It was more sixpences the men were concerned with, not less nystagmus.

When Johnson showed this report to the Lodge secretary, he challenged only one fact : that the incidence of nystagmus was not particularly high among his workers. The man seemed to have no sense at all that he had misrepresented his case in the first place by suppressing any mention of the financial interest involved.

This little episcde, and one or two others like it, made Johnson realise that it was unwise to take statements from these men at their face value. It was not that they were liars : it was simply that their attitude to anything arising out of their work was so strongly subjective, and so strongly conditioned by a hundred years of negotiations with their employers, that facts had come to be regarded as weapons of significance only if they could be turned against the enemy. Johnson, trained in academic reverence for facts, found this highly distressing. Moreover, it meant that, in building up his understanding of the industry, he could rely only upon first-hand evidence. He decided to begin by doing a shift of work in the pit.

This was no easy matter to arrange. To begin with, it was illegal. The Coal Mines Act and the recent Training Order laid it down that no one was to work underground unless he had been through a prescribed course of training.

The Colliery Agent, too, thought there was something distinctly fishy in a Ministry official wanting, not merely to visit the pit, but actually to work in it. Then a good deal of equipment was necessary in the way of suitable clothes, kneepads, safety helmet, water-bottle and bait-tin. One by one Johnson overcame these obstacles.

" What is the worst cavil in the pit ? " he asked the men in the Club.

" Third East Hutton," they told him promptly. " There's nee worse in the county."

" Who's in it this quarter ? "

" Norman Kelso and his marrows," they told him.

Norman was the big, broad-shouldered, silent and hard-drinking son of old Tom. He was reputed to be one of the hardest workers in the pit, who, with his team of self-elected workmates, was prepared to take on the hardest ' bargains ' provided the price was fair enough. (This matter of ' bargains ' was another complication that Johnson had only recently become aware of : some of the more difficult workplaces would be as it were put up to auction by the management every quarter, and teams of men would compete with each other in offering to take on the work at whatever tonnage-price they thought would pay them.) Slow-moving, good-humoured, simple, Norman had a good share of his mother's gentleness ; and it was something of a relief to Johnson to know that, if he was to do his first day's pitwork in the worst of places, he would be under the wing of the best of men.

Norman was working foreshift when arrangements were finally completed ; a bus left the village at half-past one in the morning to take the shift to work. There was a tremendous to-do in the Kelso household when Tom and Norman and Johnson came back from the·Club that night. All the equipment that Johnson had collected for the occasion was laid out on the sofa, and checked amid shrieks of laughter from the girls. Only Mrs. Kelso did not laugh

much.   The sight of so much brand-new pit-gear reminded
her how, one after another, she had seen her three sons go
off to the pit for the first time, and of the fears that had
gripped her on those occasions.   She became reminiscent.
She told Johnson how, when the boys were still young,
she would stand in the doorway and watch them as they
clumped off manfully in their heavy pit-boots, steeling
herself against the impulse to cry.   " I was allus afeart for
the bairns," she confessed softly.   Then her memories
went further back still, to the first days of her marriage.
Her father had been an official at another pit, doing soft,
easy work, so that she had grown up with no idea of the
really exhausting nature of pitwork.   Tom was nineteen
then, a hand-putter, pushing the full tubs from the face
to the haulage points and bringing back the empty tubs,
and working an eleven hour shift.   In the first days of her
marriage Tom was so exhausted when he came home at the
end of a shift that he would stretch himself on the hearthrug
the moment he came in the house, still in his sweat-sodden
pit clothes, and sleep for hours on end.   It frightened her,
for she had never seen her father do this.   She suspected him
of having some awful illness, and spoke to the village doctor
about it.   But he reassured her by telling her stories of boys
who came back from the pit and slept thirty hours on end.

As she murmured on, Johnson could feel the old lady's
gentle protective impulses reaching timidly out, blurring
the distinctions between kin and not-kin, embracing him
too, as though he were not a casual stranger indulging a
day's curiosity, but a son about to start on a lifelong career
in the dark treacherous galleries underground.

" Tha mun bide here to-neet, hinny, an' Ah'll set thee
awhee in t'morning," she insisted.

So Johnson slept for a couple of hours on the sofa in the
living-room, and at one o'clock Mrs. Kelso came down,
with a coat over her nightdress, and made tea for him, and
put sandwiches in his bait-tin.   Then she stood in the

doorway as he too started off down the long dark street, with other clumping shadows emerging from neighbouring doors.

The night began with a spectral quality. On the street corner, in the crowded colliery bus with its wooden seats, in the pityard, pale remote-seeming faces loomed into and out of small pools of thin light, with dense clanking shadows all round. Somewhere a burly shadow attached itself to Johnson, and it was only some minutes later that he recognised Norman. Men and things seemed to have lost their solidity, to have become figments in a weird industrial dream. Men murmured greetings, and he murmured back. At the window of the lamp-cabin he was given a caplamp. In a dim stream of figures he stumbled across the littered pityard and up some iron stairs, pinheads of light from other lamps swaying ahead of him. Forty feet above the ground, in a sheet-metal shed, was the entrance to the cages. Here someone gave Johnson an identity-disc, explaining that it would enable them to know who to look for if he failed to come up again. It was chilly, and the clothes of the men had a dank, sour smell as they stood waiting silently for the cages. Signal-bells clanked out messages from the shaft-bottom almost continuously.

Johnson was surprised to find, after that breath-taking journey down in an iron box jammed between five other men, that it was much brighter at the immediate shaft-bottom than on top. They came out of the cage into a place that was high and broad, with whitewashed brick walls, lit by ordinary electric bulbs. As he waited to be searched he said to Norman, whom he now saw clearly for the first time since he had started out, " If it's all like this I won't mind."

Norman grinned, and nodded towards the tunnel that stretched away dimly ahead of them.

" Save yer breath," he said, " ye'll need it when ye're inbye."

They were waiting for some men to come down in the next cage, and Johnson found himself talking to an official with a statistical turn of mind. The colliery employed just over a thousand men, the man told him. They were now four hundred feet below the surface. The pit was nearly ninety years old—new for this part of the world. The royalties covered an area of thirty square miles. There were more than fifty miles of main roadways underground.

Then the other men arrived and they started off, Johnson in the rear. For the first ten minutes the roadway was still broad and high enough for the most part to enable him to walk upright. The electric bulbs overhead, at intervals of ten or fifteen yards gave a barely sufficient light. Foot-thick wooden beams supported the roof, and here and there a splinter break in the middle of a beam illustrated the tremendous pressures exerted by the earth from all sides. Iron tracks ran down the centre of the road, and once a long line of empty tubs rolled noisily past them, hauled on a steel wire. The road got rapidly lower, narrower. The overhead lighting came to an end, and thick shadows settled round them, punctuated by the swaying soft olive-coloured lamplights of the men ahead. An occasional jar on his helmet warned Johnson to keep his head down, that the height of the roof was becoming very uneven. He began to sweat slightly, for the pace set by the men ahead was a fast one. The floor, too, was becoming very uneven, with pools of deep mud between the sleepers ; he had to vary his pace from step to step. The roof was forcing his head down lower and lower for longer and longer stretches ; occasionally the roof would open up for a few yards, and the relief at being able to straighten up for a yard or two was tremendous. The electric battery hanging on his hip became a weight to reckon with. His kneepads hampered him. The air was warm and stale, an unchanging current that only half-dried the sweat on his forehead and produced a sticky discomfort. He was glad when another line of tubs came along, and they had to withdraw into a recess while it passed.

" Is it much further ? " Johnson gasped.

Norman laughed.   " Man, ye're only just startin'."

They came to a crossroads where the roof heightened and they could walk upright for a precious half-minute.   Tub-tracks curved into the main tracks from several directions, and there were three or four men at work here.   A well-lit cave nearby housed a subsidiary winding engine.   It was like coming upon a populous little village after a night-journey through barren lands.   Johnson began asking questions, the purpose of which was to provide an excuse for loitering.   But the other men of their team were already out of sight, and Norman trudged right on without doing more than utter a brief greeting or two in passing.

He had chosen the lowest of three roads open to them. The roof was now an uneven four feet in height.   Johnson was beginning to suspect Norman of showing off before him, he was setting so fast a pace.   And then three men, travelling effortlessly with long loping steps, passed by them, going in the same direction ; and he realised that the miner was in fact going slowly out of consideration for him.

They came to a place where the end of a conveyor-belt was delivering a trickle of coal into tubs standing beneath it.   There were a couple of lads in attendance.

" They're awhee then," Norman said.

" Aye," one of the lads said, with a half-grin at Johnson. " Five minutes since."

The coal was coming from the place they were making for.   The other men on Norman's team had started work already.   This cheered Johnson, since he assumed they were now practically at the end of this exhausting journey to work.

Now they left the road where the tracks ran, and turned into a gallery where the conveyor-belt ran alongside them with a rustling sound like a shadowy underground stream.

The average height of the roof here was three feet, although at places it dropped to two feet six. On the floor was anything from three to twelve inches of thin soft sucking mud. Bent double, Johnson found himself slithering at every pace ; and each time he slithered, he grazed his backbone against the steel straps supporting the roof. After five minutes he found that the only possible mode of progress in this tunnel was to plunge forward recklessly, making no effort either to avoid falling in the mud or hitting the roof.

They were now travelling through the actual coal-seam itself ; coal formed the side walls of the gallery, save for the lowest part, where the tunnelling had been carried down into the underlying stratum of stone to give additional height. It seemed to go on interminably, this 'gate,' as Norman called it, and it took ten minutes of this desperate scrambling on all fours before Johnson saw lights ahead. By that time he was feeling that, if the gallery went on for another twenty yards, he would faint. Every muscle in his body was shrieking in protest. His head was one dull ache from incessant banging of his helmet against the roof. The skin had been rubbed off his spine all the way down his back. But now at the end of the road, it broadened and was cut another eighteen inches deeper into the underlying stone, so that he could stand almost upright. There was a pile of planks against a wall. Johnson sunk on to it, his legs thrust out, his head back against a prop, his eyes shut. He gulped desperately at the warm, stale air.

" Aye," he heard Norman say placidly, " ye'd better rest awhile before yer start work."

As soon as he had recovered sufficiently, he began asking questions.

" How far have we come ? "

" Aboot three an' a half mile," Norman told him.

" How long did we take ? "

" Aboot an hour an' a half, Ah reckon," Norman said.

" But we went slowly, didn't we ? How long do you usually take ? "

" We usually reckon ta do't in just ower the hour."

" Are there many working places as far inbye as this ? "

" Aye, they's one or two more in t'Brockwell. But they's not sich clarty travellin'. This is the worst travellin' in t'pit."

As he recovered, Johnson looked about him. The mothergate, in which he was resting, opened out directly from the end of the gateroad to the size of a long low room. Even here, where a couple of other men were working at the conveyor junction, and there were other lamps around beside the two he and Norman carried, the light was so feeble that it was difficult to see what was happening ten yards ahead. It was a minute or two before he noticed the horizontal slits in the walls of the mothergate, one on each side, from which a man would occasionally appear, the olive glow of his lamp lighting up the gap for a moment and allowing a glimpse of pitprops, and a conveyor-belt sliding past, and beyond a confused darkness of fallen stones. With something of a shock Johnson realised. These slits were the actual coalfaces, from which the coal was won.

Johnson sat there, trying to fit these slits, this darkness, into the technical knowledge of mining he had recently been aquiring from textbooks. It was clear that the method of extraction in this particular district of the pit was by what the textbooks called the ' retreating longwall ' system. As he had read about it, illustrated by nice, neat little diagrams, the method had seemed delightfully simple and intelligent. You drive three parallel roads out from your main haulage road to the edge of your boundary (that last low hellish stretch he had travelled would be one of these, he realised : in the diagrams it would be represented by two neat little lines). You would thus have two pillars of coal lying between three roads, each about forty yards wide. These you would extract from 'faces' cut at right angles to the roads, starting at the boundary, like bails on a cricket wicket. As each cut of coal was removed the faces would 'retreat' back towards the haulage road, leaving the strata above the extracted coal to cave in behind them. The advantage of this method of working was that the 'goaf,' or caved-in areas, was always ahead of your roadways, and never around them. It made for increased safety. The disadvantage, as the textbooks put it, was the initial cost of driving long roads before obtaining any output of coal. For this reason only the more far-seeing managements adopted this method.

Looking about him, in a darkness chequered by the glimmer of pitlamps, Johnson tried to appreciate that what he saw represented in some sense technical initiative and progress.

Norman, handing him a shovel, interrupted these reflections. There was work to be done. Johnson scrambled stiffly to his feet, removed his jacket and hung it on a nail, and followed his companion to one of the slits in the wall.

He found himself crawling between symmetrical avenues of props over loose coal and mud in a space less than two feet high and perhaps eight feet wide. The previous shift had cut and fired the face to a depth of four feet six, and the task of this shift was to 'fill' off the loosened coal on to the conveyor. Except where it had already been cleared away, this loose coal had spilled over into the path between the props, leaving only a foot or so of space through which to wriggle like a worm. Little pieces of this coal got between Johnson's kneepads and his knees, causing excruciating pain. A fine haze of dust filled the space, and the light of his caplamp hung on it, never penetrating beyond the next pitprop. Alongside him the conveyor belt ran smoothly, with little creaking noises, carrying a steady stream of coal away. Once he passed a man, naked save for his shorts and kneepads, lying on his side hammering a prop into place : in the dim circle of light his eyes stared wildly out of red rims in an otherwise completely black face. The man grinned a fierce nigger-minstrel grin as he passed, and only by his voice did Johnson recognise a man he had drunk many a pint with in the Club. Norman's face, too, was completely black when he caught up with him, with the same wild-eyed, red-rimmed stare— he himself now looked much the same. It was a disconcerting thought.

Now Norman began to shovel the loose coal on to the conveyor, and indicated that he should do likewise. By some habitual cunning of his burly limbs, the miner seemed able to shovel away comfortably in a kneeling position, and yet keep his head and back so low that neither scraped the roof. Johnson found that this position was far too painful for him. He cleared a little space for himself and sat, but this threw the full weight of the loaded shovel on to his arms, and before he had put more than a hundredweight of coal on the belt he had to rest. He tried sitting on one leg. He tried lying on his side. All positions seemed equally unendurable : he could only rest one set of muscles by straining another set. After ten minutes he was so utterly exhausted that he had to lie down full length in the black slime.

Lying there in the darkness, Johnson looked back over a crowded career of social investigation and thought of all the hard work he had done. He had always considered himself a hardy man. He had worked in factories at tasks considered gruelling, and been commended for his work. He had double-trenched a garden all day and felt only pleasantly tired. He had tossed hay at harvest time and been scarcely more harassed than the labourers he had worked alongside. But this—this was different. It was like trying to do any of those other jobs while chained down by heavy manacles. He watched the other at work, and marvelled. Norman, his black muscular body glistening in the olive-coloured light of his lamp, worked easily and quickly, crawling about with the agility of a mole. There was, too, an urgency behind his work that seemed almost unnatural. His shovel drove forward and cast back not only in a steady rhythm, but a fast rhythm. When he had to hack away a bulge on the face where the shots had not broken the coal off cleanly, his pick bit into the mineral with a flail-like rapidity and the full weight of powerful shoulders behind it. It was full-blooded, unrelenting and unflagging effort, that would have seemed wholly admirable in a man working in the full light of day ; down here, in the darkness of a two-foot seam, it was almost unbelievable. And yet, Johnson could obscurely sense, it was the appropriate, probably the necessary rhythm of work here. Where bodily comfort was out of the question, there could be no half-way effort : one either worked in a sustained, tearing fury, or not at all.

Johnson noticed that, even while Norman was working furiously, he always seemed to be keeping an alert eye on the roof above him. It was this that reminded him, for the first time since he had been underground, of the actual physical dangers of mining. Sometimes the miner would lay down his shovel and pick away gently overhead, prising away at a crack in the stone until he had flaked away the fractured piece which might, as larger areas of roof were exposed, fall and prove deadly. As often as the loose coal had been cleared away back to the face for a couple of yards, he would put in a fresh prop, cutting it down deftly to exactly the right length so that it could be driven home, firmly upright, to give maximum support.

After an hour or so of ineffectual efforts to use a shovel, Johnson abandoned it as unmanageable, finding it easier to deal with the coal with his bare hands. To prise out of the mass a lump of coal weighing at most ten pounds, drag it past the props and heave it painfully on to the conveyor, was as much as he could manage. Sometimes the belt would stop, jammed somewhere along the face; and then, while Norman attended to the roof or the timbering, he would collapse with his head against a prop, exquisitely grateful for the rest. He found himself feeling grateful for the dust and darkness; they at least hid something of his weakness from the other men. A deep, passionate concern with time possessed him, an anguished yearning for the minutes and hours to pass and release him from this ordeal.

At sometime during the middle of the shift he crawled down to the mothergate with the other men, and rinsed his throat with water and ate his sandwiches. The men were kindly and encouraging. " We'll mak' a pitman o' thee yet, hinny," they told him. And when he rubbed his sore knees they told him about the swollen knees miners get sometimes, and of their homely remedies, such as rubbing in methylated spirits. Johnson hoped they would go on talking there for half an hour or more; but each man, as soon as he had finished his bait, put his tin back in his pocket and returned to work. Soon only he and Norman were left. Then Norman went. With a sigh, Johnson rose and forced himself back to the coalface.

But after that break the work did not seem quite such unmitigated agony. His frame was beginning to adjust itself to the cramped, unnatural conditions, and he even managed to use his shovel for a few short spells. Most of the loose coal had now been cleared away, and the new face, clean and straight and shining in the light of their lamps, stood ready, four and a half feet from where they had started, for the next shift. At last the moment came when there were already enough men working on the little that remained to be done; and Johnson followed Norman down the face for the last time. The fear that had been nagging at him—that he wouldn't be able to last out the shift—had proved unfounded. He had stayed for five hours in that two-foot slit of earth. He had shifted between one and two tons of coal. He had done it, and he would never have to do it again.

The other men had each shifted an average of ten tons. In seventeen hours time, after two more shifts of men had brought forward the conveyor, undercut and fired another length of coal, and finished a number of ancillary tasks, these same men would return and shift another ten tons of coal each. Day after day, month after month, year after year.

Now there remained only that agonising journey back through more than three miles of ink-black tunnels. But returning the going got progressively easier; this time Johnson too managed to do the journey in not much more than an hour. At the shaft-bottom, seven and a half hours after he last saw it, he drained the last dribble of water from his can, and thought longingly of beer.

A few minutes later he was blinking in the sudden blinding spilth of morning. He stood for a few moments on an iron bridge thirty feet above the colliery yard and realised that he was seeing the place in daylight for the first time. The twinkling pulley wheels above him looked almost too small to carry their loads. Gaunt sheds of corrugated iron and small dingy brick-built offices were scattered below him in unplanned confusion, between stacks of pitprops and dumps of rusting engine parts, knit together by a tangle of railway lines. Sheer in the background of the unsightly yard rose the slagheap, a dead grey mound higher than the pithead itself, etched massively against a bright sky. It was the product, the whole scene, of ninety years of hand-to-mouth industrialism. Only the clean, bright new grace of the pithead bath-and-canteen building, erected out of the Miners' Welfare Fund, belonged to this age.

Norman, grinning, jogged his elbow.

" Awhee, man, dinna ye want some tay ? "

Twenty minutes later Johnson, bathed and changed, stood in queue by the canteen counter, enjoying his first cigarette of the day. As he neared the tea-urns he found himself standing beside a poster on the wall. It was a Ministry poster, calling for More Coal for Victory. Now, what bloody fool sent that out, he wondered ? Doesn't he know that the men only sit around in the canteen *after* they've done their work, and not before ?

He had a sudden distasteful vision of his colleagues in the Ministry offices sixteen miles away, who at that moment were just removing their hats and coats and sitting down to their desks and the morning's correspondence.

Then, with a shock of shame, that vision called up another memory. That poster. He had sent it out himself, three or four days earlier.

Chapter Three

THE ABSENTEE

THE rooms in the regional offices were large, but there were not enough of them. In the two years of its existence the Ministry had ramified like a young hothouse vine. Each of the two main directorates—Production and Labour—had met each successive administrative problem of any magnitude by the simple expedient of creating a new department to deal with it. Johnson himself was a new experimental ' department.' They had labelled him Industrial Relations and charged him with the task of spreading the gospel of co-operation on both sides of the industry. He shared his room at the Ministry with another department called Absentee Procedure.

The officer in charge of this department, Johnson's room mate, was Tom Corbell—an elderly man with iron-

grey hair and deep-set eyes. Like all the officers of the
Labour Directorate, with the exception of Johnson, he was
an ex-miner and trade union official.

He was not an easy man to get to know. Intelligent,
educated in the hard school of W.E.A. classes and books
read doggedly between shifts, he had a defensive cast of
mind, and a slow aggressive manner of speech. He
mistrusted Johnson, as he seemed to mistrust everyone
who was not a miner. He had a tendency, in conversation,
to stare through him and speak as if he were not an individual
but a hostile public gathering.

" What," Johnson would ask, looking up from his pile
of pit production committee minutes, " is a swolley ? "

Tom Corbell would place his hands with deliberation on
the top of his desk, as though about to rise from his seat.

" You people," he would say, choosing his words with
great care, " you people all think coal lies nice and level.
Well, I can tell you, if you get a swolley on the face. . . ."

" Yes, Tom," Johnson would interrupt, " but what is a
swolley ? "

After five minutes of haranguing, he would get the
information he was seeking : a swolley is a small roll or
depression in the coal seam. But it was information bought
at a price, for with it would come stories about unjust
price settlements in pits, about the swolleys Tom Corbell
had worked in, about the time he quoted Plato to the
manager, about the need for nationalisation. Tom would
forego no opportunity to state his principles, and the experience on which he based them.

Tom's duties were to administer the elaborate machinery
devised to check absenteeism. He had working under him
some half a dozen investigation officers, all of them ex-trade
union officials, who spent their time going round from
colliery to colliery adjudicating at absentee tribunals. These
men, with their intimate knowledge of the miner and his
work, were admirable at dispensing a rough and ready

justice, acceptable both to the men and the management. Johnson found that one of the most valuable aids to his understanding of the industry was to accompany the investigation officers on their rounds.

The tribunals were usually held in the manager's office at the colliery. These offices, the real administrative centres of the mining industry, nearly all looked alike, and furnished Johnson with his first real insight into the basic inefficiency of the pits. Small, dingy rooms, with wagons shunting up and down outside grimy windows, equipped with faded brown old-fashioned office furniture, rolls of plans on racks on the walls, and usually a smoky black stove for heating, it was scarcely credible that the manager of a pit employing anything up to two thousand men should have to work in such primitive conditions. A row of bell-pushes on the desk, and a couple of ancient hand microphones, were likely to be the only evidences of progress installed since the pit was first opened. But unimpressive though they were on the score of efficiency, they made a homely, informal background for the tribunals.

The investigation officer would take his seat at the desk, his dossiers before him, the manager on one side and a representative of the men's union on the other. One by one the offenders would be brought in.

Nearly always they were lads in their teens or young men. Nearly always they had been absent on a Monday or Saturday shift. Nearly always they made the excuse that they had been ill, but hadn't thought it bad enough to go to the doctor and get a medical certificate. Just occasionally a group of five or six lads would be brought in on a charge of obstruction or indiscipline.

The manner in which the investigation officers handled such cases never failed to impress Johnson. They were breezy, man-to-man, canny, but always firm. They conducted their enquiries in dialect, making acute use of their knowledge of the pits to probe behind unsound excuses.

If a lad tried to shift the blame for his offence on to a work-mate, a sharp appeal to the fairness and solidarity of miners would usually put an end to the attempt. The remarks that accompanied their verdicts were never highfalutin, and seemed to express not so much an official judgment as a communal agreement. When the record of the offender was not too serious he would be sent away with a brief warning :

" Awhee, lad, get thasel' doon t'it and dinna let me see tha faaice agin."

For cases meriting punishment the investigation officers had only one penalty : they could, if the culprit were willing to accept their jurisdiction, impose a fine of one pound recoverable if the offence was not repeated within six weeks. The whole procedure was a voluntary one, established by agreement with the owners' and miners' associations. But few indeed ever objected to being dealt with in this way. For the most part they would sign the Truck Act Book cheerfully to give permission for the fines to be stopped from their wages. Much of their willingness came from the knowledge that the forfeited fines all went to the support of aged miners.

It was an attractive, democratic method of dealing with the absentee problem. The voluntary acceptance, the informal surroundings, the working class adjudicators, the simple dialect proceedings, the union representative there to see fair play (he was paid a shift's wages by the Ministry), the fine that went to the old folk if it wasn't recovered—this was a sort of justice the miner could understand and accept. Particularly as the only alternative was prosecution in the ordinary police courts under the Essential Work Order. Tom Corbell and his investigation officers were loud in its praise. They enjoyed administering the new Absentee Procedure.

But Tom enjoyed it rather less than his subordinate officers. He only rarely adjudicated personally at the colliery tribunals ; most of his time was spent in the office, arranging time-tables for the other officers, and making out prosecution briefs against miners who had repeated their offences too often to be dealt with again by his officers.

One day Tom looked up from his papers and across at Johnson in the opposite corner of the room. He had a slightly puzzled frown on his face.

" Sam Forgan, of Tanthope. Wasn't that one of the men you took up with you on that trip to London ? "

" That's right. I'm living above him now. What's wrong ? "

" Absent from work three times in the last week without excuse. Yet he must be a pretty good worker if the Lodge picked him out to go to London."

" One of the best ! " Johnson said firmly. " But a moody sort of chap—up and down all the time. Bit too fond of gambling, perhaps. I'd be lenient with him if I were you. I'll try and find out what's upsetting him."

Johnson had not seen much of Sam in the past week— the young miner had been working on foreshift, and was usually sleeping when Johnson got back from the office. The two of them had settled down to an odd kind of relationship, governed by Sam's regularly alternating moods. For a week Sam would be almost excessively friendly, coming up to Johnson's rooms to look through his books and talk at large about the war and the pits and his gambling adventures, and sometimes even about his wife. Then, for the next few days, he would turn suddenly sullen, going out of his way to avoid Johnson, or, if he could not avoid him, greeting him abruptly and awkwardly, and avoiding conversation. It was fairly obvious that the cause of the sullenness was Sam's uncontrollable jealousy, but Johnson was at a loss to explain its periodicity until Sam himself, in the Club one night, shamefacedly told him. It was at the end of a long Friday night session, when both had drunk more pints than were good for them.

" Man, ye've bin wunnerin' aboot me, why Ah act sa queer-like, ha'en't yer? Ah tell ye. It's th' neets, man, th' neets Ah'm on foreshift. It's na good ye tellin' me ye wouldna look at ma Jeannie. Ah knaw that, man. Ah knaw ye've got a wife o' yer ain that ye love sairly. But the minute Ah leave the hoose, man, aal that divvent mak' any difference, see? There's Jeannie alane in oor part o' the hoose, an' there's ye alane upstairs. Ah knaw it's daft, but Ah canna help it! Maybe when Ah get a bit used ta t'idea Ah'll be better. But Ah dinna want ye t'take offence noo, will ye? "

All this was said with a shamed, good-natured sincerity that was completely disarming. Johnson patted Sam's hand with a semi-drunken affection.

" I'll move if you like, Sam, though I must confess I don't want to. Would you like me to move? "

But that idea positively alarmed Sam. " Ah'd nie forgi'e masel', " he said earnestly. " They's nie call for that, nie call at all! If it worn't ye, 'twould be anither. Ah mun learn t'control masel'. "

So the situation rested like that : it was understood that, while Sam was working foreshift, he could scowl and prowl as much as he liked without giving any offence, making amends during his week of backshift work. It all sorted fittingly and amusingly with the general childlike quality of Sam's character, and the fact that the poor Jeannie, frail cause of these complications, was herself such a childlike slip of a thing. Johnson, although his lips twitched uncontrollably at moments, did his best to respect Sam Forgan's strange obsessions. During foreshift weeks he kept out of Sam's way as much as possible.

A couple of evenings after Tom Corbell told him about Sam's absences from work, Johnson brought the subject up over a drink.

" I see you lost two or three shifts last week, Sam, " he said by way of opening. To his surprise Sam scowled.

" Ah s'pose Jeannie told ye that, or did ye wait up listenin' fer me t'gan oot ? " he said sullenly.

Johnson tried to laugh it off. " Now, now, Sam ! It's the wrong week for that kind of talk."

But Sam finished his beer at a gulp, got up and walked out. Johnson shrugged, and moved across to another table. An absentee tribunal was being held at the colliery the next day. In the morning Johnson had a word with the officer who was taking it, and in the evening he heard that Sam had been let off with a caution. After that he thought no more about the incident. It became merged in the general problem of absenteeism, just one cypher in a statistical table that was assuming ever more and more importance.

The miners had just been given a large wage increase, stabilised by Government agreement for four years. The owners were prophesying that the men would be less inclined than ever to work, now that they could earn as much in four shifts as they had previously earned in five. To prove it, they were watching the absentee figures like hawks. Every other day a Group Production Director would storm into Corbell's office, excitedly waving a sheet of paper.

" Look here, Corbell, you've got to put a stop to this ! Have you seen these figures from the Maizie pit this week ? Scandalous, absolutely scandalous. If your officers can't do better than this, we'll have to prosecute, that's all ! "

These G.P.D.s—there were six of them—had until recently been chief agents or directors of the bigger colliery companies in the region. They still retained their offices in their undertakings. But now they were civil servants, paid by the Ministry to give technical assistance and advice to groups of other collieries as well as their own. It was hoped that this scheme of grouping the collieries, and appointing a production director from the largest under-taking in each group, would eventually facilitate amalgama-

tions.   Meanwhile they were being very energetic about
absenteeism.

So were the colliery managers, who sent in bitter letters
complaining that the Essential Work Order deprived
them of any disciplinary powers.   So were the Chairmen
of Directors, whose letters in the *Telegraph* and *Mail*
demonstrated that if you gave miners an inch they would
take a holiday.   So were the mine-owner M.P.s, who put
down incessant questions for the Minister about the rising
absentee figures.

Each of these separate pressures, gathering weight as
it gravitated down from higher quarters, focused finally
upon Tom Corbell.   Absenteeism, absenteeism, absenteeism !   The hypnotic syllables drummed incessantly, fraying
his nerves and befogging his mind.   He could not but feel
that the miners were letting him down.

" We're losing the sympathy of the public," he would
burst out.   " We'll never get nationalisation now."

Even his beloved tribunals were being threatened.   There
were proposals to increase the fines, to lengthen the period
of probation, to have automatic recourse to prosecution
after three appearances before an investigation officer.
The word ' prosecution ' particularly was coming to be
heard almost as often as the word ' absenteeism ' itself.

Johnson tried to soothe Tom Corbell.   " It's all part
of the campaign, Tom.   They won't touch your tribunals—
they're too useful to them."

" What do you mean—useful to *them* ? " the ex-trade
unionist demanded aggressively.   " The owners'd have all
the absentees in the police courts to-morrow if they could.
That's what *they* want, not tribunals."

" I'd be surprised if they were that stupid," Johnson
said mildly.   " The tribunals help them to get prosecutions,
if that's what they want."

It was one of Tom Corbell's proudest boasts that the
number of prosecutions brought against miners in the

courts had fallen considerably since his tribunals had been established. This was true. But, as Johnson pointed out, a closer reading of the figures also showed that the number of convictions obtained had actually increased.

"The fact is, the local magistrates regard your tribunals as something that sieves out only the worst cases for them, so they're more ready to convict now," he said.

This was another thing he was learning about the industry—the need to scrutinise its figures with extreme care before basing any argument upon them. There never was such a statistically-minded industry; it was possible to get statistics about every aspect of it (except capital investments: when a Cabinet Committee wanted to get statistics on this subject in 1942, in order to fix a standard rate of profit, they failed). All discussions revolved round percentages, every battle became a statistical battle. And especially the Battle of Absenteeism.

Johnson studied the absentee statistics with particular care. He found two things wrong with them. The pre-war percentages had been based on a five-shift week. Since 1940, however, the industry had gone over to a six-shift week, and this was now used as a basis for absentee percentages. Thus although the miners were losing more time, it was of a bigger total. The amount of time they individually spent at work was not appreciably less than before the war, when their wages were low and there was much unemployment.

But the percentage was a rising one, the Production Directors pointed out angrily when Johnson told them of his discovery. And the percentage had risen appreciably since the new wages agreement.

That was the second thing wrong. Just at the time the new wages agreement was introduced, the first Bevin Boys were coming from their training centres to the pits. Many of them didn't like the pits: they left without warning and could not be found for months, remaining meanwhile on the colliery books as absentees. It was impossible to discover how much of the increased absenteeism was due to absconding trainees, but certainly an appreciable amount of it could be so dismissed. What remained, in actual absenteeism, struck Johnson, with his experience of other wartime industries, as remarkably small.

In face of these facts, to emphasise absenteeism as a major problem of the industry was sheer irresponsibility.

It was easy enough for Johnson, of course, with a job sufficiently above the battle to allow detachment, to see through these specious clamouring demands to reduce excessive absenteeism; but Tom Corbell, constantly attacked from every side, the assailable harried by the unassailable, could only become more worried, bewildered and uneasy. This, after all, was something the miners *could* do: work. They themselves could take this last excuse from the owners, and leave them naked in their incompetence.

" The older miners are doing their bit all right," Tom would say fiercely. " Men my age, we never get any trouble from them. It's the young ones. They're the lazy ones, they're the ones who take shifts off. If the older men can go to work regularly, the young ones can too. They're letting us all down ! "

He would brood over this. " I don't know what's come over the youngsters. They won't go to the Lodge meetings, either. All they think about is dogs and pictures. They leave everything to the old men now."

Johnson would timidly remind him of the social history of these young miners. They had been brought up during the depression years. They were just beginning to sit up and take notice as the pits were beginning to close down. They had been fed at school, most of them, because their parents hadn't enough money to feed them at home. The coal that burned in their grates came from the slagheap, not from the mine. The picture they had unconsciously absorbed of pitwork was one of desolation, humiliation, grinding poverty. The wonder was that these young men should consent to work in the pits at all—not that they should occasionally take time off.

But there was in Tom some deep, almost religious sentiment about mines and miners that could not accept such excuses. " Miners have been through rough times before," he would say grimly, " but they've stuck by their unions. These lads are letting their marrows down."

In some degree or other, Tom Corbell's bewilderment was shared by all the ex-trade union officials in the Ministry. They had all much the same history. They had worked in the pit and in the union. They had educated themselves aggressively, in order that they could the better fight the owners. They had been checkweighmen, Lodge officials, battling daily for their cause in the colliery office, in the local council chamber, on the district arbitration boards. They had lived through the 1926 lockout and the lean years following. They had lived by, and drawn strength from, the myth of the nationalisation to come.

And then, in 1942, the Government had set up the Ministry to take over operational control of the industry.

They saw it, every one of them, as the first step towards nationalisation. They told themselves and their men that if this partial control could be made to work, then it would prove to the country that nationalisation was possible. With the approval and backing of their union executives they accepted the invitation to join the Ministry and administer its labour policy, feeling that by doing so they had nothing to lose and everything to gain for their cause.

Coalowners, on the production side, were doing the same. Their nominees, or the nominees of mining machinery companies, filled all the technical posts.

But what the ex-trade union officials had not clearly

foreseen was that in practice operational control of the mines would prove something very different from control of mining operations. The machinery of administration that took shape in the Ministry's first year followed the line of least resistance. Distribution was easy to control. So was the supply of mining equipment. So, with union men and union backing, was labour. Into these channels all the energies and talents of the administration flowed—particularly into the control of labour. There were hundreds of new schemes introduced to regulate or discipline or placate labour : rehabilitation schemes, medical schemes, transfer schemes, training schemes, hostel schemes, clothing schemes, schemes for withdrawing miners from the armed forces, schemes for optants, schemes for prosecuting strikers, schemes for dealing with absenteeism and (this was were Johnson came in) schemes for explaining these schemes to the people affected.

But of schemes for improving the technical capacities and functioning of the mines there were remarkably few. On this side the Government's White Paper programme had become virtually inoperative. The reasons were, quite simply, legal.

In the first place the manager of a coal mine is legally responsible for the safety of the mine and the people working in it. And safety considerations are indissolubly bound up with every mining operation. Any manager could therefore refuse to obey any direction issued to him by the Ministry on the score that he was not satisfied as to the safety factors involved. -

Managers may choose to disobey a Ministry : they will not often disobey their boards of directors. Could not the Ministry issue its instructions to the directors of the undertakings, and leave them to secure the compliance of their managers ? Alas, no. Legal decisions on the Defence Regulations made it obligatory for the Government to finance any new development schemes involving the use of an undertaking's credit. The Ministry could not order an inefficient pit to change its methods of working without being prepared to pay for the change.

The Production Directorate had therefore only the most indirect powers—even if it wanted to make use of any. It could act negatively, in opposing an undertaking's labour requirements or orders for equipment; but could only 'advise' in matters requiring more positive action. Small or poor undertakings, those that would have liked 'Capital Assistance' from the Government, were more dependent on the Production Directorate's goodwill: but even this financial power was very limited, for in four years of war the Treasury had sanctioned only £4½ millions in expenditure of this sort, a good proportion of which had gone to the bigger and more powerful companies.

Apart, then, from investigating and approving schemes requiring the outlay of public money, there was very little for the Production Officers to do. The miners saw very little of them, and were keenly suspicious of what they did see. For these were the men who, tackling mining problems in order of tractability, spent their surplus energies deploring the rate of absenteeism.

In these circumstances, the Production Directorate could rub along quite nicely with the owners. But not so the Labour Directorate with the men. The Tom Corbells were finding that the miners increasingly associated them with fines and prosecutions and attempts to uproot them from their native village and transfer them to another miles away. All the compulsions exercised by the Ministry were done in the name of the Labour Director. It was small wonder that the men, remembering his trade union past, should evoke the classic image of the beggar on horseback.

Now, in the second year of their civil service tenure, the Tom Corbells were beginning to ask themselves uneasy questions. For years they had worked to establish a position of leadership among their men—had they lost that now? And if so, what had they got in its place? Would the Ministry survive the war? If not, what would be the use of all their administrative experience if the men distrusted them?

Now they were beginning to hedge their bets. They went out unofficially at week-ends and made revolutionary speeches to Lodge meetings to prove to the men they were still on the side of the angels. When a parliamentary seat fell vacant in a mining constituency they engineered their names on to the selection committee's lists. Rumours of a job going in the Welfare Commission or Coal Commission would set them busy reviving old contacts. For an ex-trade union official, the Ministry was beginning to look like a good place to be out of.

As the summer came on, the campaign against absenteeism gathered intensity. The Invasion of France produced a slight check in the figures, but not as much as might have been expected. Some of the pits were taking their holidays that week: others were due to have them in the two or three weeks following. It was traditionally a bad time for work. Some men, working at different pits, liked to have their holidays together: the fact that the pits closed for different weeks led to many men taking a few days off to share a friend's legitimate cavortings. The situation this time was further complicated by the somewhat tactless appeal for those pits which had not already taken their holidays to forego them in view of the Invasion. Many Lodges interpreted this as a covert attack on the newly won right to a week's holiday with pay every year: they replied that they would forego the holiday if the owners paid them double time during that week. More public sympathy was lost by this seemingly mercenary attitude. Appeals to the miners to produce more coal became daily sharper in tone.

Prominent among the absentee-baiters in the Ministry

was Major Salter, lately chief agent of the company which owned Tanthope Colliery and now a Group Production Director. He was an elderly man, tall and silver-haired, with a patina of beautifully mannered courtesy overlaying the brusque, commanding habits of his early military career.

Major Salter came rarely to the city offices : he was a country man, who did his work largely by telephone from his lovely Queen Anne house in the hills a mile or two beyond East Tanthope. He ran a boy's club at Cannock-dene, another pit owned by his company, and his wife was very active in village affairs. He liked to have it thought that he knew intimately the family life and history of every one of the five or six thousand workers employed by his undertaking. He kept a close watch on the names of absentees submitted by managers of pits in his group, and would send little commentaries on the characters of the men from the pits he was best acquainted with, for the guidance of the investigation officers. These commentaries usually took the form of a scribbled sentence : " Won £30 at the greyhound races last week," " A bad lot—got a girl into trouble last year," " Drinks too much." These titbits he had picked up at third- and fourth-hand from his club-leaders and his wife, and Johnson was amazed how wrong he frequently could be, at least so far as East Tanthope men were concerned. When Sam Forgan's name appeared on one of these lists for a second time, for instance, Major Salter wrote against it : *Thoroughly lazy fellow, shirks his Home Guard parades.* Sam was exempted from Home Guard duties because of his mutilated hand.

It was, on the face of it, a somewhat sinister habit, but it was in fact no more than a naïf expression of the Major's rather feudal concern for the well-being of his men. His picture of the ideal mining village was strangely like Tom Corbell's : a virtuous, hard-working community, where the women went regularly to chapel and the men went regularly to their Lodge meetings, where folk got married at an early age and brought up large families. Owner and miners' leader, both deplored all activities running counter to this pattern of life. Drinking, dancing, cinema-going, gambling—such things, made ever more available by the growing transport system linking the colliery villages with the city, were disrupting the sober settled ways of the mining community. Tom Corbell was sufficiently alarmed to see nothing wrong in Major Salter providing him with information about any individual's predilection for these destructive vices ; if he made no use of it, it was only because he was well aware of the Major's little habit of getting his information wrong.

The Major never tried to supply, nor would Tom have tolerated any attempt to supply, information about the political affiliations of any man.

There was another little habit of Major Salter's which was not quite so engaging. He was an impassioned believer in the efficacy of ' making examples.' Regularly he would announce his theory that the way to end absenteeism was to select the worst offender of the month and prosecute him in the police courts. He did not stop there. Every month he would comb the absentee records of his group of pits, select the man who in his opinion was the worst offender, and demand that the Ministry issue a summons against him. At a time when Bevin Boys were absconding from the pits daily, and magistrates all over the country were straining the law to be lenient with them, it was not feasible to comply with the Major's demands. The sole effect of this was to make each successive demand rather more shrill than the last.

It was a shock to Johnson when he learned, late in the spring, that Sam Forgan had been nominated as Major Salter's ' prosecution of the month.' It appeared that Sam had lost seven shifts in six weeks, all without reason-able excuse. Other men, it was true, had lost more, but they had taken the trouble to cover themselves with medical certificates. All this time had been lost during weeks when Sam was on foreshift.

A combination of late working and deliberate avoidance had kept Johnson out of touch with Sam's emotional history in recent weeks. Now, he decided, he must thrash out this absurd and bizarre situation. That same evening after he had read Major Salter's report, he bought some bottled beer and half dragged the reluctant Sam up to the privacy of his rooms. The young miner sat in one of the meagre armchairs, his blackened, shapeless hands grasping the wooden arms, his face comical with tangled shames and suspicions. Johnson poured beer and asked questions.

Phrase by phrase, with many angry splutters and incoherences, the miserable little story unfolded. It was the story of a marriage. Sam had met Jeannie at the dances at the Miners' Welfare Institute; she was very fond of dancing. She had been going with another lad then, a garage hand, and during a quarrel with this young man she turned to Sam for consolation. Afterwards she made it up and Sam was dropped; she didn't want to walk out seriously with anyone who worked in the pit, she said. But two months later she found that Sam had got her into trouble, and so she came back to him. They got married almost at once; but Sam could never forget that Jeannie would have preferred to marry the garage hand—not because she loved him more, but because he wasn't a miner. Since then Sam had always been acutely jealous of non-miners, where his wife was concerned. And now that he had a non-miner living over the top of him, he could not rest.

Truly a miserable and absurd story, which, presented as an excuse for absenteeism, would be hooted at by any right-minded investigation officer. But it had two effects on Johnson. First, he decided that he would have to move out of the house as soon as ever he could make alternative arrangements. Second, it brought dramatically to his notice one of the deeper consequences of the failure of the mines to keep pace with the general progress of the times. If in a world dedicated to conspicuous consumption young miners were finding that their work lowered them not only socially but sexually as well in the eyes of women, then it was certain that recruitment to the mines would fall rapidly. How important a factor was this in determining the rapid deterioration of the industry in the past twenty years? What other, equally unobvious social factors were at work in the same way? What could be done to minimise their consequences? After this evening of intimate talk with the young Sam Forgan, Johnson found his mind crowded with questions which he was incapable of answering.

In his office next morning, like a good civil servant, he dictated a long memorandum on the immediate need for a thorough social survey to be carried out in the coal-field, with special reference to the social factors underlying absenteeism, indiscipline and restriction of output.

Chapter Four

THE MANAGER

THE dozen or so really large and modern collieries in the region were all in the eastern parts, strung out fairly evenly along the coast. The reasons for this were geological. The coal measures, outcropping in the western foothills, ran out under the sea to an unknown distance (they were believed to be workable to a distance of ten miles from the coast, although no one had yet got that far); but near the coast a layer of running sand, bearing almost unlimited quantities of water, interposed itself between the coal-bearing strata and the thick upper cover of limestone. The limestone and sand together made a water-bearing layer of anything between sixty and eighty yards thick, and to sink a shaft through this required technical ingenuity and financial resources both of some magnitude. The first efforts made to sink shafts along the coast, in the first half of the nineteenth century, resulted in several bankruptcies. One company found itself keeping three tanyards in operation simply to replace the leather pipes and buckets used for stemming the flood of sand and water. But in the second half of the century the exploitation of the undersea coal was made easier by the almost simultaneous development of freeze-as-you-bore methods of sinking and the limited liability company. Most of the coastal pits were sunk after the sixties.

It was one of Johnson's jobs to arrange underground jaunts for official visitors to the region; and of course such visitors had to be taken to an up-to-date pit, where they could ride to the face on ' man-riding ' sets and hew a piece of soft coal in a four-foot seam without fatiguing themselves overmuch. It was not, however, quite so disingenuous a practice as it sounds. For if visitors thus saw the work of the miner at its unrepresentative best, they were certainly given an opportunity to see his living conditions at their very worst.

There were few recognisable villages along the coast, as inland. The population was a heterogeneous gathering from all quarters of the country; the housing a product of the most miserable period of private jerry-building. The miners' cottages stretched in long unbroken miles along the roads linking the collieries, sometimes thickening into a ganglion that called itself a housing estate or a town, but predominantly just a row. Occasionally a poster or a bottle in a window distinguished one cottage from the others as being a shop; more frequently a swinging sign, and perhaps a third storey, indicated a pub; every few miles came the dingy façade of a co-op. store; and sometimes there was a tin-roofed chapel or church. But none of these things did anything to mitigate the unvarying meanness and joylessness of the view. It was as though some morbid actuary had tried to put all the squalors of the world end to end to see how far they would reach. A sprawling nightmare, spawned by the slagheaps in the background.

It was in one of these coastal pits that Johnson first met Steve Joyce. He was the manager of the New Main colliery, a small compact man in his forties, with a face riddled with small blue scars like a hewer's and hands permanently ingrained with coal. Steve Joyce had an energy and zest, a liveliness of mind and a passion for argument, and above all a kind of intellectual hospitality that kept open house for every new fact and idea that came his way, which set him head and shoulders above anyone else Johnson had met in the coalfield. He talked at the top of his voice no matter who was in the neighbourhood, and his speech consisted largely of a series of minor detonations.

" The treacherous bitch ! " he greeted Johnson the second time he met him. " The treacherous bitch ! She's farting and firing again in the third West Harvey ! But I'll clean her teeth for her, the red-fanged whore, I'll stop her stinking tricks ! "

Whenever Steve Joyce talked of whores and bitches, he had Nature herself in mind. He had an inveterately dramatic imagination, and saw his life as an incessant personal struggle against this wild incalculable adversary he had conjured out of the underground darkness. Other, subsidiary demons in his private mythology were all the managers who had preceded him in the running of the colliery, his directors, and all mining inspectors.

Once he had discovered Steve Joyce, Johnson lost no opportunity of seeking him out. In particular he contrived as often as possible to accompany Steve on his morning tours of the pits. Every morning, at half-past seven promptly, Steve arrived at the pithead in his pitclothes and visited one or other district of the underground workings. It was a colliery with an annual output of half a million tons, obtained from four different seams, the lowest of these, the Harvey seam, occurring at a depth of nearly nineteen hundred feet and, in the undersea areas, having a high temperature and a good deal of occluded gas. To accompany Steve Joyce to these lowest winnings was a truly educative experience. From the moment he stepped out of the cage at the shaft bottom and began firing questions at the onsetter, he was all eyes, ears and hands. He might be carrying on a vigorous conversation with Johnson, discussing the applicability of some American machine in a particular working district ; but constantly he was noticing the state of the roof, the amount of stone dust on the floor, the leakages in a ventilating door, or replacing a haulage wire on its bearings, checking the pressure in a compressed air pipe, the alignment of a trunk conveyor, the angle and density of a pack, the lubrication in a bearing. Anything he discovered at fault he would put right with his own hands if that were possible, chalking his initials beside the rectification so that the person really responsible could exercise his conscience over the matter. At the coal face, it was noticeable, his mind became as it were flushed with a professional excitement, as though after twenty-five years of colliery work his spirit still rose to the adventure of the front-line attack. He would crawl past the chocks into the goaf to get a close view of the point of fracture of the roof, and then, returning, exchange ardent views on the matter with the nearest workman to hand. A restless itch of experimentation would set his fingers twitching. The amount of spillage of the conveyor, the positioning of a light, the bluntness of a pick, the size and shape of a lump of coal—such small things challenged him with a thousand problems, which his mind and hands fidgeted to resolve. It was useless for Johnson to try to follow all the firefly dartings of Steve Joyce's interests down there in the heat and noise and blackness of a three-foot-six coal face. But later, on the surface, as they massaged their muscles back to freshness with soap and hot water, or sat at the canteen table with large mugs of tea, a few well directed questions would be sufficient to revive all the hopes and fears of the morning's work. Only the immediate excitement had abated now, and the day to day tactics of the coal face fell into place against the background of pit strategy.

He would talk, perhaps, about his plans to experiment with a team of men working on a short face, each team completing the full cycle of operations in a single shift. Or his project for arch-girdering the gate-roads. Then, gulping down his tea, he would say, " Come on over to the office and we'll get the plans out—you'll be interested in this ! "

Pit plans, with their superficial planlessness, their little meshes of thin lines interspersed with great irregular patches of shaded areas, their coloured arrows, their arbitrarily distributed geological conventions, their pencilled additions, were always things of mystery to Johnson. Even when he had learned, in a superficial sense, to extract some meaning from them, his mind could never fully accept the fact that this thin black lane, perhaps a quarter of an inch long, represented that dark fissure a third of a mile below ground where half-naked men by the dozen sweated and panted in the light of Davy lamps. It was typical of Steve Joyce that, when Johnson once made some remark to this effect, he revealed that he had already given a good deal of thought to this very point. " You're right," he said, " it's limited information you get from even a large-scale plan. That's why I go home and make myself a plasticine contour model when I'm planning a new development. There's a hell of a lot of professional snobbery about mining plans. Lots of managers feel there's something vaguely shameful about admitting that they can't visualise all the conditions of a district from the information given on a plan. But I know a good many haulage roads in this county—or in this pit even !—where the gradients and the ventilation would have been easier if the manager had messed around with a few pounds of clay before he laid them out ! "

But the plans of the New Main colliery suffered, not only from the general defects of all mining plans, but from shortcomings of their own, for which his predecessors in the management of the pit were responsible.

" God help them, the catchpenny knaves ! " Steve would bellow from time to time. " Look at these Bensham seam workings ! See it ? Easy coal and cheap reputations, that's all they ever thought of. See all that lovely coal out to the south of the boundary—I ought to have a good straight main road out to it. But no, there was some easy coal nearer the shaft, so out it came, sixpence a ton cheaper than the next man's, and everyone said how efficient ! "

And then his furious finger would follow a line on the plan zig-zagging through shaded areas of worked-out coal.

" So I have to drive my haulage road anyway I can through their waste, and keep a gang of stonemen constantly repairing it ! It's enough to break a man's heart—it's like that in every seam ! Twenty-two managers there've been in this pit before me, and not more than half a dozen have tried to see more than five years ahead ! No plan ! No professional pride ! Just miserable price-cutting and carpet-bagging ! "

Complaints of this sort were common, of course. Johnson heard similar stories from most of the managers he talked with. But it was true he had never seen working plans quite as chaotic as these. The truth was that the New Main pit favoured such practices. It was one of the oldest of the big coastal pits, owned by an *ad hoc* undertaking representing finance corporations. The company had had bad luck with the sinking, which had cost a quarter of a million more than was anticipated, and had not ventured, as later companies owning coastal royalties had done, to sink further pits.

From the point of view of the ambitious colliery manager, the one-pit company was becoming increasingly a dead end. For large companies, with several pits, were appointing ' agents,' either to superintend various technical aspects of their business, or to co-ordinate the day-to-day working of sub-groups of collieries. Under this system the manager of the mine, while retaining his responsibilities under law, was tending in fact to lose real power and status. It was no longer the final prize for a colliery manager to be appointed to a bigger and better pit— that had become just one stepping-stone to a well-paid job as agent to a bigger and better company. The New Main company had no such jobs to offer. Their pit had therefore become a place for the ambitious manager to demonstrate his fitness for an agent's job elsewhere, by proving that he could increase output and reduce costs. Having done so, ruthlessly, he would pass on, leaving for his successor an accumulating legacy of planless workings.

" But to what extent *can* you plan ahead in a colliery of this size ? " Johnson asked Steve Joyce. " I mean, for how long a period and in what detail ? "

" Well, let's take the basic facts first," said Steve promptly. " When this pit was opened it had reserves of more than a hundred million tons of coal—plus an unknown quantity of undersea coal beyond the three-mile limit. The drawing capacity of the pit is about half-a-million tons a year—though of course that could be stepped up if we wanted to. Allowing for seventy per cent. extraction, that gives the pit a working life of at least a hundred and fifty years."

" But obviously you can't plan that far ahead."

" To some extent you can. There're a number of things that hold good no matter what changes in technique and economics take place in a hundred and fifty years. Space, air and light, for instance. No matter what else happens, the more of them you have, the easier it'll be to get coal. And all three depend ultimately on having good straight main roads. So from the outset it can be laid down that, within your geological conditions, good, straight broad haulage ways and airways should be available right out to the furthest edges of your boundaries. And no development that makes good roads more difficult should be tolerated."

" But it's asking a lot for a coalowner to expect him to forego an advantage now in order to make coal-getting easier in a hundred and fifty years' time ! "

" Agreed. That's why I speak only of preventive planning for such a period : it isn't in fact asking much to ask that a pit shan't be murdered. My point simply is, that from the point of view of a colliery manager—and the nation too, if it comes to that—the natural period of planning is the natural term of life of the pit. The owner's natural period is much shorter. It's the natural term of life of the capital he puts into the pit. That raises difficulties about fixed and working capital, of course—but let's take the average amortisation period and add a few years for good measure : let's say thirty years. Is that too long a period for positive planning ? Take old John Frain. who was working this pit at the outbreak of the last war— what could he have foreseen about to-day ? He'd have been misled by the fact that the natural output had gone up by more than fifty per cent. in the previous thirty years. He couldn't have foreseen the collapse of our export trade, and the depression. He'd have expected me to work out the Bensham seam by now. He'd have expected me to be well out to sea with the Hutton and Harvey. He'd have expected me to be much further from the shafts in all directions than I am now. Therefore he'd expect me to have two major problems—ventilation and travelling times. Well, he might have been inclined to over-estimate them a bit, but in the main he'd be right. He'd know that the best help he could give me would be big arched airways with as few gradients as possible and as few unnecessary bends. He'd know that the further out I got, the more I'd think in terms of man-riding sets, and therefore I'd want plenty of height on my haulage roads. He could have foreseen all that quite clearly, even if he couldn't have foreseen anything else. And I can foresee that the man who'll be running this pit in thirty years' time will want those things even more badly than I do !— But John Frain wanted an agent's job along the road, and got it ! So I have to use a couple of hundred horsepower more than I need to get air to the faces, and seventy or eighty men too many on the haulage roads."

" But if the market's good, and the sales agent hands the manager a contract for quick delivery, what's to be done about it ?

" What's to be done ? " Steve Joyce had a ready and passionate answer for this question. " The first thing to be done is raise the professional standards of the colliery manager ! Give him the pride that you find among doctors and lawyers ! Why, if there were only a dozen men in this country who'd rather throw up their job than associate themselves with short-sighted, dangerous and dishonest scrambling for output—why, that in itself would almost revolutionise the coal industry ! "

" But aren't you laying too much blame on the manager ? "

" God forbid ! But I'm proud of being a colliery manager. I think it's the grandest job in the world ! And it riles me when I go to Association meetings and find so many men who don't ! "

" But the sort of managers you have is largely determined by the sort of policies companies pursue. What can be done about that ? "

" One thing that can be done is to keep these bloody utilisation chemists in check ! That's been one of the worst effects of the scramble for markets in the past twenty years—the way every little Tom, Dick and Harry with a Lancashire boiler has been taught to order his coal on a chemical formula. Some of it is a good thing, of course, in so far as it's taught people not to waste a good coal where a bad one will do. But too many companies have gone in for it as a smart form of advertising : you know the sort of thing—' you be our customer and we'll give you *exactly* what you want, with an ash fusion temperature of sixteen hundred degrees centigrade ! ' The result is that hundreds of pits have to work more seams than is really necessary, to meet phony specialised demands. I know one pit not far from here where they have an output of 1,200 tons a day. To get it the manager works eleven districts in six separate seams, and has nearly thirty miles of main haulage roads to maintain, with six separate haulage systems. He's got three hundred men working on haulage alone : one to every four tons of coal produced. All because of chemistry ! With a rational marketing system, he could get the same output with two haulage systems, ten miles of road and eighty haulage hands."

" That's interesting. But for the last three years the markets have been only too pleased to take what they're given. And at the same time the Government has been asking for concentration in the most productive seams.

What has prevented that colliery from closing up four of its seams ? "

" Because you've got to offer some inducement to the company before it'll close a seam that it might have to re-open in a couple of years anyway. Underground roads are expensive, and if you leave them standing unattended for a couple of years they cave in. To close four seams would mean a real loss of fixed capital. Mind you, it would be well worth it if the company knew that the markets were going to continue to take whatever coal they're given. But the chances are that after the war the markets will get more and more discriminating, not less. The new plastics industry, for instance, is very choosy about the coal it uses. And with the development of its by-products, the gas industry is also getting very choosy. Take me, for instance—I've got a coal that's very rich in hydro-carbons, but has also got a fairly high sulphur content. The Italians bought quite a lot of it before the war. But so long as there's a chance of a pit along the road producing an equally rich coal with a lower sulphur content, I'm not going to put all my eggs into that one basket. You can't stampede me into patriotic concentrations in wartime unless you make it all right with my directors first."

" But if it weren't for your directors you yourself would prefer to concentrate your production into one or two seams ? "

" In some ways, yes. But not just to get more output. In normal times, if I increased the efficiency of this pit, I wouldn't produce any more coal, I'd just lay some more men off. There was no point in producing more coal, because I couldn't sell it. People'll buy less, but they won't buy more of the damned stuff than they can use. The productive capacity of this country is approximately 330 million tons a year—it's gone up ten per cent. since before the last war. But the industry can only sell about 250 million tons a year. We can produce our share of that without being very efficient, because with price-fixing schemes and one thing and another our standards of efficiency are set by the worst collieries, not by the best. That's the odd thing about this industry—it doesn't obey any of your economic laws. There are at least a score of pits in this county, for instance, that have been worked continuously since the eighteenth century, and are now working their last little pockets of two-foot coal miles from the shaft. According to all the rules, when the Castlereagh Colliery opened up twenty years ago, with its three-quarters of a million tons a year output, at least a dozen of those old inefficient pits ought to have been forced out of business. But they weren't. They don't make much, but anything they make over their labour costs and running costs is profit on two hundred year old capital. They're the pits that set my standard. If you want to start concentration schemes, start with them. Introduce an efficiency test, so that no pit can employ labour unless it can run six days a week, paying a good minimum rate, and still produce coal at current export prices."

" Cut out excess capacity, eh, Steve ? It's an old solution, and there's an old objection to it. The coal these inefficient pits work is valuable to the nation, and we haven't got so much of it that we can afford to leave it unworked."

" Complete nonsense ! In this county alone there are 700 million tons of coal left unworked to support roads and buildings. There's another couple of hundred million tons left as boundaries between royalties. After you'd redistributed the royalties, the few odd million tons you'd lose by closing down the old, inefficient pits wouldn't be noticed. And meanwhile think of the saving in terms of men's lives ! Before the war, every pit, efficient or inefficient, had a body of men dependent on it for work. The industry always had a quarter of a million men on its books for whom it couldn't find work : men with no other use than to help us managers enforce discipline

and keep down wages. Those old pits kept thousands of
men hanging around with only a ghost of a chance of
providing them with a full week's work : it wasn't the
men, but the pits, that were being subsidised by the
dole."

"Everything you say seems to lead directly to state
intervention. Yet the history of the industry in the past
thirty years seems to suggest that state intervention usually
fails. The Government control of the last war sent
output down. The temporary subsidy of 1925 only
postponed the lock-out of 1926. The price-fixing schemes
of which you complain so bitterly were the result of the
1930 Coal Act. And now once again, in this war, Government control is achieving nothing."

"Failed ? From whose point of view ? Any action
Parliament takes is either for the advantage of the owners
or the miners. They're the only two groups with an
effective lobby. The consumer's interests aren't considered, because the consumers aren't represented as such.
It's only from the consumer's point of view that state
intervention has failed. The '25 subsidy benefited the
miners. The 1930 Coal Act benefited the owners. Both
wartime controls have greatly benefited both sides.
They've even, in a way, benefited me."

"But the purpose of the controls wasn't to benefit
anyone. It was to raise the production of coal."

"So you put the county in charge of a man who
admittedly doesn't know the first thing about the production of coal, you give him a production director who is
a director of a powerful combine, and a labour director
who is the nominee of the unions ? I don't see how
a set-up like that can be expected to increase production."

"The theory is that they'll behave like ministers in a
coalition government—sink their differences for the duration
and work together to win the war."

"Oh, they'll do that all right—on the surface ! And

they'll *try* to do it thoroughly. But you can't be surprised if they frequently get confused about which war they're trying to win! After all, the owners and the men have been fighting their own private war for a hundred years or more. It's been a more violent, bitter and exhausting war than most people realise. All the customs and traditions of the industry are those of warfare. It's instinct with the miner to oppose every move of the owner. It's instinct with the owner to oppose every move of the miners' union. The war hasn't brought anything new into the mining villages to help break down those deep-rooted habits of thought—apart from a few Bevin Boys. The war with Germany just gives both sides the chance to give a new patriotic twist to their old fighting slogans. The miner says you can't get more coal unless you national-ise the mines. The owner says you can't get more coal unless you reduce wages."

" And what about the colliery managers ? "

" The war has changed things a bit for us—in some ways better, in some ways worse. But remember first of all that this present generation of managers has been trained in a pinch-and-scrape, cost-cutting atmosphere in which we all got a lot of practice in ' making do ' and no practice at all in being efficient. We'd learnt to rely on cheap labour and plenty of it—and now you make labour expensive and scarce. That's put most of us out to sea. For years we'd only got to put a notice up at the colliery gate to have skilled men walking ten miles to get a job—and now you expect us suddenly to learn to be tactful, to take pit pro-duction committees into our confidence, to be patient with trainees. That's the hard part of war for us. The easy part is, that we've now got a chance to tidy our pits up a bit."

" For God's sake ! The Ministry, the country is dunning you daily for more coal, and you talk of tidying up your pit a bit ! "

"Exactly! I'm a technical man. I know how my pit *should* be run. But I never had a chance to run it properly before the war. Now you come along and set me a 'Target' based on my highest pre-war output. You know damned well that output was achieved in an atmosphere of cut-throat competition, with every cost cut to the bone. Now you've put a ceiling on the company's profits, but you haven't put one on costs. So my directors aren't keen to eat up their reserves, and to me it's a heaven-sent chance to put back into the pit some of the things I've been robbing it of all these years. I can drive that haulage road as I've always wanted to, even if it costs a few more pounds to do it. I can enlarge this return airway and scrap that one. For once my directors don't object. It's true my output goes down five hundred tons a week while I'm doing so, and I sincerely wish it didn't. But for me the really important thing is to improve my pit."

"You know it sounds pretty paradoxical to say that ouput is deteriorating because the pits are being improved."

"I'm not saying that's the only reason why it's deteriorating. But you know enough about pitwork now to know that, within fairly narrow limits, to-day's output is determined by last year's and the year before's development work. And after all, it shouldn't be such a mystery to you : the same thing happened in the last war. With a hundred thousand men in the forces, the industry kept up an output of 250 million tons a year. When the Government took over in 1917, output immediately dropped by twenty million tons—in spite of the fact that we got most of the men back by that time. And output stayed down till the Control was lifted in '21. Yet when the boom came in '23, it was possible to step up production suddenly to practically the highest pre-war figure. Every mining man knows that we couldn't have done that— an eight million ton increase in this county alone !—if we hadn't put in some very good development work during the control years."

" It's a little hard to reconcile your statements with the fact that the Ministry finds it very difficult to persuade colliery owners to mechanise their pits. . . ."

" Ah, machinery! That's a different matter. That's capital equipment. That's something you can't charge against the Guaranteed Wages Fund. And you can't just monkey with mechanisation schemes. If you introduce a power loader at the coal face, you've got to bring the transport system behind it up-to-date. Mind you, there's nothing I'd like better—any sensible manager who looks at his wage-bills these days must be all for machines. But if the pits are nationalised after the war, I'll stay here, and my directors won't. They're not going to spend their good money on machines now if there's any chance of the pit becoming Government property in 1948. They're reluctant even to replace existing machinery —every time I ask for a new air compressor I'm told to hang on to the old one for a bit longer. The only way you'll get mechanisation schemes going now is to persuade the Treasury to pay for them. And even then you'll have to keep a sharp eye open to see that what you're paying for really is a mechanisation scheme. I know one company that's preparing a nice £35,000 scheme which it hopes the Ministry will pay for. The only essential difference between this scheme and the pit's normal method of working is in the longwall faces retreating instead of advancing. Any real modernising that's likely to be done in this coalfield in the next four years will be paid for by the Government, mark my words. Uncertainty about the future of their pits doesn't inspire coalowners with any spirit of adventure ! "

These views of Steve Joyce's were not delivered in any one single talk, but in a series of conversations and arguments extending over weeks. They were biased views, of course, for although Steve liked to think that his position as manager put him above the struggle of industrial politics, his very passion for technical efficiency involved him more than he knew. Labour was one of his technical problems : he was therefore not inclined to blame the workers for being problematic any more than he blamed a wire rope for having a breaking point. Economics and finance he regarded as his directors' problems : and when these ran counter to his technical interests he could not help feeling that his directors weren't doing their job efficiently. Thus in most issues he was inclined to excuse the miners rather more readily than he excused the owners.

Because of his zeal for efficiency, one of the landmarks of Steve Joyce's wartime experiences had been a visit which the American delegates of the Joint Resources Board paid to his pit during their tour of the coalfields. He never tired of repeating a story illustrating American conceptions of efficiency and our own. One of the delegates had stood at the pithead for a long while, watching the coals being drawn to the surface. He noticed a man sitting in a little cabin making entries in a book.

" What's that guy doing ? " the American asked.

" He's the checkweighman," Steve told him.

" Checkweighman ? What's that ? "

" He's a man appointed by the miners to check our weighman's record of the tubs."

" How do you weigh the tubs, then ? "

Steve explained that a weighman was employed to record the weight of each pair of tubs as it passed over an automatic weighing machine. Any serious deficiency in weight was debited against the man or team of men who had filled the tub.

" Couldn't you have an automatic register to do that ? "

" Of course we could. But the men would think we were trying to get rid of the checkweighman."

" But I guess the idea is to get rid of both of them."

" The union fought bitterly for years for the right to appoint a checkweighman. He represents a major victory for the men. They pay his wages themselves. If I did anything that seemed to attack his position, I'd have a strike on my hands."

" But an automatic register would be fairer, and save the union good dough at the same time."

" I'd still have a strike on my hands."

A glazed look came into the American's eyes, and he asked no more questions during the course of the visit.

Three or four months later, when the report of the American commission was received, and its publication deemed 'inadvisable,' Steve Joyce was on tenterhooks until Johnson managed to read a copy in the London office and was so able to convey to him the heads of the Americans' criticism. They had made it quite plain in their report that they took a pretty poor view of the British coal-mining industry. They had complained about the lack of any awareness of the urgency of production on all hands, and had specifically included Government officials in this indictment. They had found ventilation and lighting, even in the best pits, very bad, and the haulage and transport systems primitive. They had also criticised the short hours worked by the miners.

" Knocks all round, eh ? " Steve Joyce commented almost with relish. " No wonder they wouldn't publish it ! That's an interesting bit about the miners, though— of course the American miner does work longer hours than ours : but that's because of our lousy roads and ventilation and lighting. You come back to my old slogan : plenty of space, plenty of air, plenty of light. Then, too, the Americans haven't got this fantastic tangle of safety regulations growing year by year and poisoning the industry like a upas tree. Look at your Mining Inspectors ! They all know that the essentials of safe mining are good roads and good ventilation. But do they use their power to improve them? Not a bit of it! They ignore fundamentals and seize on superficialities. They'll accept the statutory minimum of ventilation, but fuss about with complicated safeguards to prevent explosions. They'll accept miles of travelling roads so low that by the time the men get to the face they're too exhausted to have all their wits about them in case of danger—but they'll wag their heads for weeks over the remote risks of riding the men inbye on the conveyor-belts. And what's the result? Mining machinery is crusted over with a ravel of costly devices till they're getting to the state of the pre-historic monster—so safe they won't function. So the manufacturers cease to try to sell their machines on their efficiency, and sell them on their safety. When one manufacturer wants to put a competitor's nose out of joint, what does he do? He adds yet another gadget to his machine, sends it to Buxton—where the officials are bound to support anything aimed apparently at greater safety— and gets some stooge manager to try it out. Then he only has to interest an inspector or two in it, and they go round saying that 'so-and-so's' gear is much better, and orders are diverted to the new model. Whereupon the other manufacturers do likewise. So the margin of efficiency between machine-mining and slave-mining is reduced, costs are cut on fundamentals in order to pay for inessentials, the whole industry is further depressed, and the manufacturers of machinery end by subsidising collieries in order to have a market for their gear!"

Closely linked in Steve Joyce's mind with his diabolical Mining Inspectors were the trade union leaders who sought to curry favour with their men by securing increments of 'danger money.' This was a subject on which he was apt to become almost incoherent with anger.

"Danger money!" he would explode, "Danger money! Coming into this office and asking me to pay a man sixpence a shift extra to kill himself in my pit! And mind you, they'll get quite affronted when I tell 'em I employ miners to dig coal, not graves. God ! if ever there was a pernicious thing it's paying danger money to miners ! It makes the men accept almost any conditions provided they get a few extra shillings for it ! It corrupts the local officials, who know damn well they'll get little thanks from the men if they demand improved conditions, but pints all round if they can blackmail the manager into choosing between another tanner a shift and some fantastically expensive gadget ! And it can easily corrupt the manager, who's got enough temptations as it is, God help him ! '

Always, after returning from a session with Steve Joyce, Johnson would find himself wondering just how reliable he was as a witness. The man's very virtues made it difficult to decide. Johnson did not know another manager in the coalfield so passionately interested in mining efficiency as such, or with his intellectual range and ardour, or so ready to talk freely and frankly about his work. He stood out among the run of managers in the county as quite exceptional : indeed it was one of his own frequent sources of complaint that he was so exceptional : " It's a third-rate industry," he was fond of saying, " and it's only attracting third-rate brains." But for this very reason much of his conversation had an almost dilettante flavour. Few of the ideas he developed so vehemently could be tested against facts, or other people's ideas, because his own opportunities, and the practice of the coalfield, were so narrow and limited. His pit was well-run, his output was good though not startling, and his incessant little experiments to get better results with the equipment avail-able kept him more than fully employed. But the eagerness with which he welcomed Johnson's visits, the long letters which Johnson would find on his desk the morning following these visits—letters amplifying an argument or point of view which Steve feared had not been adequately covered in discussion, these things indicated an isolation of the mind in which an idea can unwittingly be welcomed for its nonconformity as much as for its correspondence with fact. It was unwise, perhaps, to lean too heavily on Steve Joyce for an interpretation of the industry's problems—without, at least, checking his key statements.

Chapter Five

THE SECRETARY

JOHNSON'S knowledge of London hot-spots was limited and out-moded, but it sufficed to ingratiate him with the young buck on the Production side of the Ministry whose job it was to follow up complaints made by the pit production committees.

At the age of twenty-six, young Trunder had exhausted the social possibilities of the county. "One roadhouse within a fifty-mile radius," he would say disgustedly, "and even that closed for the duration!" If the climate of war made him chafe at the lack of gaiety around him, the letters he received from his undergraduate friends in the forces, writing about the hectic leaves they had been spending in London, exacerbated his discontent. By way of compensation young Trunder had developed an insatiable curiosity about metropolitan night life.

It was, from Johnson's point of view, a useful weakness, and he was thankful for the twenty-year-old memories of Kate Meyrick and Sergeant Goddard which enabled him to exploit it. For Johnson's position in the office was an odd and incertain one. Among these Northern colleagues of his, 'practical men' one and all, he had a rather irrelevant and accidental air, like a chessman intruding into a game of draughts. At first his southern 'standard English' accent had made him an object of suspicion among the men on his own side of the Ministry ; and only when he had succeeded in convincing these of his good intentions did he realise that, by doing so, he had widened the gulf between himself and the Ministry's technicians. For the Production Directorate was unobtrusively but unmistakably aware of itself as the gentlemanly side of the Ministry. All its officers had university training and manager's certificates. They played classy games and belonged to the ' only decent ' club in the city. They were careful to take their lunch at different restaurants from those patronised by the Labour people. Having neither a gun nor a bag of golf-clubs, Johnson might have remained for ever beyond the pale if it had not been for young Trunder's odd interests.

The advantages of being on good terms with Trunder were many. He spent a good deal of his time underground, making inspections of haulage layouts and air compression installations and whatever else the men were complaining about. He also had a fast, throaty open car, which could take him from one side of the county to the other in little more time than it took to go twenty miles by bus. As the son of a ' safe ' colliery agent, managers would talk uninhibitedly with him. In young Trunder's company, Johnson could get to outlying pits, view their workings and talk with managers off their guard, all with a minimum of effort. With a coalfield of five hundred square miles to cover, such things were important.

Trunder lived up in the fells of the western side of the county, and it was in this direction, by preference, that he would turn the nose of his car. In these parts, as one drove out of the city following the river inland for a few miles, then climbing southwards through the wooded foothills with an arrowy little trout stream flashing first on one side of the road and then on the other, it was easy to forget that this was coal country. The pitheaps were kept low, and merged easily into the contours of the hills ;

the miners' rows were older on the whole and fashioned
of a native stone that fitted the character of the country-
side. The very coal itself changed with the changing
scene. In the west, all but the uppermost measures produced
an exceptionally fine coking coal, and most of it was owned
by two large companies with their own iron foundries
and coke ovens close at hand to the pits. Suddenly, in a
fold of the romantic hills or a bend of the flashing river,
one would come upon these little pockets of incongruity—
a black country scene of belching blast furnaces and smoke
stacks, railway sidings and slag—or a new plantation of
council houses with street-names like ' Lenin Avenue '
and ' Karl Marx Road,' with a pit-wheel twinkling in the
background. Then the fells would close in again on the
road, farms and woods and moorland heather, and young
Trunder, slowing down to let some cattle pass, would
take up his rake's catechism where he had left it.

" What went on in the back room at Smoky Joe's ? "

" Did you ever see the Prince at the Forty-Three ? "

" What happens in a raid ? "

With the virtual monopoly of some of the finest coking
coals in the world, the two companies dominating this part
of the coalfield had been left comparatively unscathed by
the depression. This distinguished the mining villages of
the west. Remote and self-contained, theirs were stable,
hard-working, comparatively prosperous communities. In
the depression years they had had the lowest unemployment
rate in the north. Now they had the lowest absentee rate.
Methodism was still a living force in these villages. The
pitmen, undistracted by city lures, read more widely and
thought more soberly than most in the county, were
disciplined in their industrial behaviour and adventurous
in politics and local government. Their delegates to the
County Mineworkers' Association formed a solid radical
block, sticklers for established principles, slow to advocate
strike action, concerned with long term rather than short

term policies, yet with a stubborn conservative streak where matters affecting old traditions and customs were concerned. These villages had given the Association some of its most outstanding leaders.

The collieries of the west presented a less pleasing picture. They were large and old—some of them had been supplying the local foundries during the armaments boom of the Napoleonic wars—and they had long exhausted their thicker seams : much of their best coal was now being won in seams of eighteen inches or less. Hand hewing and pony-haulage was still the dominant method of working. Comparative freedom from competition had enabled these collieries to resist most technical advances save those in which their captor-undertakings had a direct interest. Thus steel arch-girdering took the place of timber wherever possible, giving the main roads a great air of modernity ; while the conveyors used on the longwall faces, instead of being the rubber belt affairs so obviously called-for in these thin seams, were the ancient scraper chain conveyors with heavy iron troughs taking most of the space between floor and ceiling—the very first coal conveyor introduced to the trade in the closing years of the last century by one of the local undertakings, and considered obsolete now by all except the director who invented it.

They were indeed interesting places to visit, these upland collieries, with their slagheaps kept low and long, unobtrusive among the woods and hills, with views from the pityard over one of the loveliest river valleys in the country. Even the workings had a strange gothic quality of their own. Many of the pits could be entered by drifts—steep tunnels cut down through the base of the hills. They would change their clothes, this oddly-assorted pair of civil servants, in the manager's office—Trunder into a highly professional rigout of blue hoggers and leather-backed jerkin, Johnson into a scratch kit of ancient flannels and a sweater: then they would follow one of the officials along a surface haulage line, with a bitter wind slapping at them from the fells, for a mile or so to the little wooden token-cabin by the entrance of the drift. Here—for these were naked-light pits—they would borrow a couple of acetylene lamps, ancient contraptions with shallow reflectors that burnt your knuckles if you did not hold them properly. Then down a long seemingly-unending flight of broad stone steps, with a miniature waterfall coursing down alongside, and a low, rough-hewn roof—two hundred yards of slippery steps, probably, before you reached the level of the workings. These acetylene lamps gave a sharper light, and threw sharper shadows, than the little four-candle-power Davy lamps Johnson had grown used to: and the multitudinous underground springs kept the air free from dust. Shambling apelike through miles of low galleries, Johnson never lost the sense that here he had slipped back centuries in time, back to the simple mining world of Agricola. Some of the seams were badly faulted: at any moment you might have to descend a twenty-foot staple—down vast stone slabs like the steps of some medieval dungeon—to another level. You would come upon a man working alone by candlelight in a new winning sixteen inches high: lying on his side, with his shoulder resting on a small sloping board, he would pick away patiently along a face of twelve yards, advancing it perhaps a foot in the course of his shift. Or suddenly, out of the darkness ahead of you, there would come a strange rattling thunder, and fierce animal eyes catching the light from your lamp; then you would press yourself against the side of the road while a pony passed drawing a tub of shining coals, with a black, half-naked youth, uttering wild yells, crouched on the limbers with his head nestling against the pony's rump. From time to time you would wade for a few hundred yards through inches of slurry, with treacherous potholes between the sleepers of the haulage rails: thousands of gallons of water had to be pumped out of these pits daily. Sometimes the iron girders supporting the roads, buckled into fantastic curves under the tremendous pressure of the earth, would cast weird writhing shadows as a party of colliers approached from another direction.

In these pits you really got the impression that the managers knew intimately every man working for them— a virtue every manager likes to claim, but very few indeed possess. They would talk with the men at the face about the week's betting or a wife's arthritis; and if the managers didn't start the talk the men themselves were as likely to. Most of these managers had been in the company's pits for thirty or forty years, were local men born and bred, speaking the same dialect as the men who worked under them, and would have felt stranger and more out of place in a big modern pit on the other side of the county than Johnson himself.

It was at a pit production committee meeting in one of the larger pits in these parts that Johnson first met Joe Colmart. He was a well-set man with a plethoric face and broad forehead: a man with a permanent worried frown. He had, in committee, a tense, brusque guarded manner, and an air of scrutinising the meaning of every word to its furthest implications before allowing himself to speak. Johnson had come to try to enlist the aid of the committee in arranging a meeting in the colliery village: he had discovered by this time that no function in a colliery village can prosper unless sponsored directly or indirectly by the miners' Lodge, and it was on the pit production committees that he could meet the Lodge officials in their most pliable mood.

Joe Colmart, as chairman of the committee and secretary of the Lodge, listened to his request with a kind of scowling attention.

" Ye say that this Colonel knaas aal aboot th'Invasion ? "

" He was with the Fiftieth on D-day and he's only just come back," Johnson assured him. " And he's had men from this county with him all the way. Probably lads from this village."

" Oor men dinna go much on propaganda talks," Joe Colmart said unhopefully. " They might listen t'a pitman from th'Fiftieth—but a Colonel." He shook his head.

" It's not a propaganda talk, it's an eye-witness account of the beachhead fighting," Johnson said patiently. " And for all I know, the Colonel may be a pitman. Plenty of colonels have risen from the ranks."

" Aye, an' pit managers too," said Joe Colmart, with a half-glance at the manager of his own pit, sitting at the table. " But that dinna mak' 'em any more popular wi' the men." There was a laugh at this, in which the manager joined.

Eventually Joe Colmart agreed to take the chair at the Colonel's meeting, and to use his influence to make the village turn out. In return Johnson undertook to engage the Lodge Crakesman—a sort of public crier who went round the streets with a big wooden rattle making announcements of public importance—for two evenings at seven-and-six a time, to advertise the occasion. A picturesque bargain, which indeed saved Johnson the bother and expense of having posters printed. But the arrangement was also an accurate index to Colmart's habits of thought. He had, inveterately, a negotiator's mind. The Ministry had approached him, for its own transparent purposes, with a proposal. He agreed that the miners might like to hear a first-hand account of the Invasion. He sincerely believed that talks of this kind could help to make it easier for him to deal with the younger men in his Lodge. But it was a proposal, and therefore he must have a proposal of his own to take back to the Lodge and present as the fruits of an able piece of negotiation. The Crakesman would get fifteen shillings out of it, and Joe Colmart had the satisfaction of having successfully fitted a new situation to an old formula.

The meeting, held in the Miners' Club a week later, was very successful. Whether because of the lusty lungs of the Crakesman, or the prestige of Joe Colmart, the little hall was packed, and the Colonel was heard, if not with enthusiasm, at least with interest.

After that episode, Johnson met Joe Colmart fairly frequently, at home, on committees, in the Ministry offices. He was, without question, the father of his people. He lived in a little cottage, one of a row of three which the Miners' Lodge had built to house its chief functionaries (fear that their organisation might be smashed by the victimisation of its officials led every Lodge to build such houses as soon as its funds justified the cost). The cottage was kept sparkling by Mrs. Colmart, who seemed to spend all her time either making pastry or clearing her husband's papers from the living room table preparatory to doing so. She was a sharp, silent woman who kept her nose out of her husband's business, although that business interfered a good deal with her own. For from morning till night, whenever Joe Colmart was home, there was a constant stream of callers. Men came to him to report that they were short of timber on their face, that their pick-steels were not being sharpened properly, that the overman was disputing their claims for consideration payments, that they wanted a permit to buy Wellingtons, that the shot-firers were firing the coal badly, that the ' flat ' needed to be advanced, that their utility alarm clocks were losing time, that the cuttermen weren't cleaning out the corvings, that the doctor had refused them a ' light work ' certificate, that a colliery house had a leaking roof, that there was too much stone in the latest delivery of coal. He was expected to advise, or to deal with, every problem that arose in the pit or the village. Apart from being secretary of the Lodge, he was on half a dozen pit committees—urgency committee, baths committee, welfare committee, production committee, aged miners' homes committee, canteen committee, social club committee, Services' cigarette fund committee. He was a member of the local and County Federation Boards, delegate to the Council of the County Mineworkers' Association, an urban district councillor and Chairman of the divisional Labour Party. Joe Colmart's life was compounded entirely of negotiations at various levels in the miners' interests, and, since he had no offices, all the preliminary work was done in the ' front ' room of his cottage, with Mrs. Colmart producing cups of tea and slices of pie for all but the most transient visitors.

Conversation with Joe Colmart was a rather trying business. He had been conducting the affairs of his Local Lodge for fifteen years or more, and in that time had had little opportunity to reflect or read or absorb new experience. Instead he had reduced the results of earlier reflection and reading to a handful of dogmas and slogans which he used to block any enquiry beyond the day-to-day range of his negotiations, and which he could pronounce with breath-taking pomposity. Some of these were amusing enough at first hearing, but when they were repeated, time after time, to evade an unpleasant fact or banish a problem, the habit became almost macabre. " When they sell coal in chemists' shops at a guinea a box, I'll be satisfied, not before." " Keep your big words for the owners—what the miner wants is a big pay-packet." " The Government will never run the mines until the miners run the Government." When you abstracted these slot-machine slogans from the man who uttered them—the well-set, sombre, homberg-hatted executive with half his mind on his next engagement—you could catch from them a far-away echo of the bitter lively young mind that had first coined them in the full horror of industrial depression. But that was fifteen, twenty years away now.

A month or so after his first meeting with Joe Colmart, Johnson was given a further opportunity of studying him at work. There was a sudden flare-up of trouble with the Bevin Boys at the local pit.

In these western parts the new mining conscripts had not been received with enthusiasm. The villages were old and settled in their habits. Few strangers came among them in the normal course of events, and they were as untouched by the culture of the towns as it is possible to be in the age of radio. Now, called upon suddenly to absorb dozens of discontented youngsters brought from distant cities to work in their collieries, they found it almost too much for them. There was trouble in the cottages where the Bevin Boys were billeted. It was said they were dirty, finicky, disrespectful, careless, noisy, irresponsible, shameful in their behaviour to the girls of the village. The lads, no less difficult to please, did their best to live up to these epithets. Some of them ran away home. Lodge secretaries were instructed by their members to complain to the Ministry about others. The Ministry pressed forward the construction of a hostel in the district.

The hostel was completed and the boys lodged in it. But if the social difficulties were somewhat eased thereby, industrial difficulties were multiplied. Removed from the restraints and influences of the miners' cottages, thrown together for their leisure as well as their work, they fed each other's grievances, their natural tendencies to 'gang up' were encouraged. They were too, few at first to do more than, sullenly or derisively, resist any demands on their interest or goodwill. They stayed in bed instead of getting up for the foreshift : they committed an occasional act of minor sabotage underground ; there were stories of hooliganism at the village dances. Above all, most of them refused to join the miners' union. It was evident that, when their numbers increased and a leader emerged among them, there would be real trouble.

In the Regional office there was much anxious scrutiny of the activities of Bevin Boys in the western parts of the county, and a tendency, among the ex-trade union officials particularly, to discuss every little peccadillo reported as though it were a major question of policy. The crisis, when it came, took nobody by surprise. Indeed Johnson was half-tempted to believe that it was as much a result as a fulfilment of their forebodings. But there was no doubt, from the rapidity with which the news spread from department to department of the Ministry, and the gasp of awe with which it was revealed, that this indeed was the crisis.

A Bevin Boy had refused to buy a lamp !

The implications of this behaviour were, Johnson was told by his colleagues, quite tremendous. It was the county custom for miners working in naked-light pits to buy their own acetylene lamps or candles, the company paying a few coppers a week for their maintenance. It was also the custom for the miners to purchase their lamps from the company, a weekly deduction being made from their wages until the price was recovered. The Bevin Boy was fresh from work in a factory, where the idea that a workman should pay for the light to work by was quite ludicrous. He also had a bosom pal who had gone to work in a gaseous pit, and was there provided, free of charge, with an electric caplamp to work by. He claimed that if his pal could be provided with light free, so could he ; that if it was dark underground, it was no responsibility of his to make it lighter. Quite simply, he refused to buy a lamp, and refused to work without one.

" If he gets away with it," Tom Corbell said bitterly, leaning over his desk to give portent to his words, " then we'll have to buy lamps for all the Bevin Boys. And if we do that, then there's ten thousand miners in this county who'll want the same treatment. There's already a lot of grumbling because the Ministry provides the lads with a safety helmet to start work with ! "

But whether by accident or not, the young man had chosen his ground with perfect generalship. He could not legally be compelled to work in the dark. He could not legally be compelled to buy a lamp. He had only to hold out, and either the company would have to provide a lamp free, or the Ministry would have to transfer him to a gaseous mine. In either event, every other Bevin Boy who had not yet bought himself a lamp would share the victory. The ultimate, horrible issue was : either the naked-light pits would have to provide light free of any charge, or they would get no Bevin Boys.

Johnson had half expected the union to lend all its support to the lad. For the issue raised the whole question of lighting in the pits. There was no doubt that the underground lighting of the mines in general was grossly inadequate. The chief technical excuse for this was that ordinary standards of lighting were unsafe because of the danger of explosions. But clearly this excuse did not apply in nongaseous pits (there were more than forty non-gaseous pits in the county), where it was perfectly in order to carry naked flames. Here was obviously the place to begin the necessary revolution in underground lighting. Instead of acetylene lamps, with their splutterings and sudden extinctions, instead of candles flickering at each slight movement of air, there could be power-lighting giving full and healthy illumination for the miner's every movement. Surely, Johnson thought, the union will seize this opportunity to raise the whole question of lighting ?

But when Joe Colmart hurried to the Regional office to put the point of view of his Lodge, it was with very different intentions.

" This," he said menacingly, " is it. An' reet glad Ah am too ! If these lads dinna join th'Union, why, man, the men'll raise hell ower this ! "

The Lodge, too, saw the issue simply. That a miner working in a naked-light pit should provide his own light was an immemorial custom, accepted by the union. If it was to be challenged, it was only to be challenged by the

Union. Therefore Bevin Boys of a challenging disposition must join the Union and accept its discipline.

" Have you asked him to join ? " Johnson asked its indignant representative.

Joe Colmart's mouth hung open in genuine astonishment for a moment. " *Ask* him ? ASK him ? " His voice rose an octave in horrified disgust. " D'ye think aal Ah've got to do is gang aroon' *askin'* men ta join th'Union ? What sort of lad is it that needs ta be *asked* ta join th'Union ? "

Johnson tried to point out that in other industries and other parts of the country the solidarity of the workers was not so fully developed as here. Recruiting campaigns were a normal activity of most trade unions. But Joe Colmart saw no reason to modify his attitude because other communities did not share it.

" Ah joined th'Union the day Ah wor sixteen," he said. " An' so did every other man in oor Lodge. We didna wait till summan cam' along an' asked us."

" Speaking off the record, Joe," Johnson put in. " What would happen if you supported this youngster ? He's obviously a bright lad, and there's no doubt it's a scandalous anomaly he's hit upon. If you supported him, it'd show the Bevin Boys that the union is really interested in them, and at the same time it's a heaven-sent chance to agitate for mains-lighting. What do you say ? "

Joe Colmart's jaw hardened. " I say that when t'miners need ta be shot o' auld customs, they'll dee it theysel's, wi'out the help o' Bevin Boys ! " he said.

The policy adopted by the Ministry after hurried deliberations on the crisis was strangely like Joe Colmart's. The young men needed trade union discipline. Particularly this trouble-maker needed trade union discipline. (It was interesting to note how some of these ex-trade union officials could speak of the workers' organisations as though they were penal institutions.) Then if they had any grievances they could make their representations through the normal channels. Ministry officials must go out to the hostels and . . . well, put the case to them. As for the trouble-maker —he was obviously a case for the Industrial Relations officer.

It was with a strong distaste for his job that Johnson went out to the hostel next day. The lad was there, an eighteen-year-old veteran of the London streets named Stacey, aggressively spruce in manner and appearance. Most of the other boys were at work or sleeping, and without their backing he was obviously feeling a little lonely and scared behind his best suit. Johnson took him across to the Workmen's Institute and bought a couple of beers.

He was easy game, of course. A few compliments, a hair-raising story or two about the miners' sufferings and struggles, an appeal to him to take over the leadership of the other recruits as a kind of unofficial commission from the Government, and he was won. Johnson took him straight round to Joe Colmart's house.

" Joe, here's Mr. Stacey, who's been causing such a fluttering in the dovecots. He wants an application form to join the union. What's more, he's going to be your recruiting sergeant in the hostel from now on. A valuable chap, eh, Joe? Just the sort of young leader we need these days. And by the way, he likes the look of the Institute billiard table, and wants to become a member there too." Johnson's voice became ,almost hysterically hearty as he saw a ponderous frown settle on Joe Colmart's face.

" So ye've decided not ta mak' trouble, eh, ma lad? " the secretary said with the accents of a magistrate addressing a repentant prisoner. Johnson flung an anguished look at him, then said with a hurried laugh, " Don't let him scare you, Stacey, my boy—he's always a bit liverish in the mornings ! " But Joe Colmart was not to be deflected from his settled course by looks or flippancies.

" Well, Ah think ye're doin' the wise thing, lad. But,

mind, if ye join the Union ye'll have ta behave yersel'. They's ta be no more o' this lamp nonsense!"

Johnson saw defiance hardening again on the youngster's face, and said with a desperate briskness, "Look, Joe, I want to catch the next bus back, and I want to have a chat with Stacey here before I go. If you give him an application form he can sign it and we'll leave you to your work."

Fortunately the role of the brisk executive was as dear to Joe Colmart as that of the disciplinarian, and without more ado he produced the document and a pen, collected half-a-crown, and closed the episode with all despatch. Walking back to the hostel, Johnson tried to assure the young man that the secretary's manner was just the northern way of showing a fatherly interest.

So the incident of the Bevin Boy and the lamp ended, not with a bang, leaving only a slight sense of guilt to rankle in the mind of a middle-aged civil servant. Nothing, of course, had been settled. Young Stacey might pay his union dues for a while, but he would be given no encouragement to attend Lodge meetings or take an active share in the life of the union. He and his kind were wanted as members only because it was a point of pride with the miners that no-one working in the mines should be outside their organisation.

An ardent unionist in principle, Johnson found himself very unhappy over the whole affair, particularly his share in it. Having spent a good part of his life trying to persuade workers to join their unions, he now found himself feeling almost like a confidence trickster because he had helped to recruit one boy. Was it, he wondered, just because of Joe Colmart's way of handling this particular situation? Or was this oldest and most honourable of unions just behaving with traditional exclusiveness? A hundred years before, when the coalowners had brought in men from other parts of the country to break a strike, the miners had collected a thousand strong and wrecked the pithead while the strangers were underground. Were the Bevin Boys of 1944 being confused with the blacklegs of 1844?

A week or two later there was a strike of deputies, which gave Johnson yet another opportunity to watch Joe Colmart and his Lodge at work.

The strike had been impending for months—ever since the new Wages Agreement. Under this agreement the wages of the vast body of mineworkers had been greatly increased, in the case of some pieceworkers by as much as twenty-five per cent. The deputies (minor officials of a status similar to that of the factory foreman) had not benefited under the main agreement, and their County Association had immediately claimed an increase under a subsidiary award to 'skilled men.' They had thereby gained a shilling a shift, but had in doing so committed themselves to accept the main principle of the agreement, that no variation in the rates awarded should be sought for a period of four years. This was undoubtedly a strategical mistake, not committed by the Deputies' Associations in other counties. In the neighbouring county, for instance, the deputies had carefully refrained from becoming signatories to the four year agreement, and had later successfully negotiated with their owners for a much larger increase.

Within a month or so the full anomalies of the situation were apparent to everyone. The deputies in this region were not only drawing wages which were often two pounds a week less than the men working under them, but thirty shillings or so less than the deputies in the neighbouring county. And they had formally committed themselves to accept this situation for the next four years.

Their leaders thereupon made another false step. They lodged a claim for an increase in wages with the district conciliation board, which promptly rejected it. They then handed in strike notices, and brought the case before the National Reference Tribunal : here too it was inevitably rejected.

The situation was complicated by the fact that the deputies in the county were divided between two associations. About one-third of their numbers were members of a special section of the County Mineworkers' Association—the union covering the great mass of the miners. The rest belonged to their own, distinct association. The miners' union had its own plan to obtain an increase for its deputies ; therefore in this dispute it instructed those of its members who were deputies to remain at work. When the strike notice expired, only two-thirds of the deputies in the county came out.

The moment the strike started, the miners' union broadcast an appeal to all lodges to ensure that production of coal was not affected by the strike ; face workers were, where necessary, to take over the duties of deputies who were out on strike. Even the least cynical of observers could not help remarking that the signal success of this appeal contrasted oddly with the jejune response usually accorded to the appeals made by the miners' leaders. Although the strike lasted more than a week, hardly a ton of coal was lost as a result. In many pits output for the week actually went up. Never was there a more ineffectual strike. It was the miners who made it so.

Never, indeed, was there a more unnecessary strike, although this was not at first apparent to Johnson. What was apparent was the subdued grin of satisfaction on the face of every official of the miners' union whom he met in the first day or two of the strike. It was very marked on the face of Joe Colmart.

" We've got 'em where we want 'em, now," he said succulently.

" The deputies ? " Johnson asked innocently. " But surely you agree they're entitled to an increase ? "

" Increase ? " Colmart waved that question aside as

without importance. " Awhee, man, we can get 'em that any time."

" Then why haven't you done so already ? "

" We wor waitin' ta see what th'Deputies' Association would do." He gave a cunning grin. " Ye can trust them ta gang the wrang way aboot anything ! Then when they boogered it up, we'll step in an' get their increase for 'em. Mind ye, we never expected 'em ta do anything sa stupid as call a strike. That plays *reet* inta oor hands ! They've nie chance o' bringin' it off wi' us agin 'em. Ye'll see, they'll lose half their membership afore we've done wi' 'em ! "

That, then, explained the prompt response of the men to their leaders' appeal. The intention was to break, not so much the strike, as the rival organisation. But why were the miners' leaders so sure they could obtain the disputed increase when the deputies' association failed ? Joe Colmart, now that events could no longer be influenced, gloried in divulging the canny secret.

The wages agreement fixed wage-rates for four years with no provision for alterations ' other than those normally made in respect of changed methods or conditions of work.' This was the only loophole for change. To secure an advance for the deputies, some change in their conditions of work was necessary. Now it was a statutory responsibility for the company to provide ambulance boxes at every working place, and it was the custom for deputies to carry these boxes in and out of the pit. A small payment was made in return. But for deputies to carry ambulance boxes was customary only, not compulsory. If the union offered to sign an agreement making it compulsory for all deputies in its membership to perform this task, the owners would jump at it. Thereby the conditions of work would be changed within the meaning of the agreement, and the way would be open to obtain the increased wage-rate. There would be no opposition to the increase itself, for

everyone was agreed that it was desirable if only it could
be granted in such a way as to leave untouched the main
principle of the agreement.

Such was the solution the mineworkers' union intended
to apply—after the rival organisation had had time to
demonstrate its inefficiency. Meanwhile the strike moved
raggedly to its predestined failure. The strikers, seeing the
pits still working at full blast, lost heart, held meetings,
returned to work. The Ministry's lawyers wondered
whether to prosecute some or all, and decided against
prosecuting any. The local newspapers wrote paragraphs
of praise for the men who had worked harder to maintain
output. The secretary of the Coalowners' Association
received a letter from the secretary of the Mineworkers'
Association proposing an agreement about the carrying
of ambulance boxes. . . .

Cunning. Blind, unscrupulous, aggressive cunning.
Ingrained and ineradicable the habits of thought that distorted every situation into the pattern of conflict, that sought
to dominate events for domination's own sake. It was
not inspiring to watch at close quarters the Joe Colmarts
of the industry at work. Walk with them down the village
street to the pit gates, hear the comradely greetings from all
sides, the incessant requests for help and advice, and you
got a quite moving picture of democratic leadership. You
saw that the union penetrated and dominated the social life
of the village so completely that it was scarcely conceivable
for a miner to have a birthday party for his son without
having a Lodge official there to make a speech. But sit
with the Joe Colmarts on a committee, have dealings with
them on any issue involving other interests than their own,
and you were shocked and perplexed by the mean, narrow
and unimaginative attitude they adopted. "They's nie
Charity in t'Coal Trade, wi'out it's Charity Maain," they
would tell you. It was easy enough to find an explanation
of such an attitude. The infamies and treacheries of

mining history were visible in every pit village. The experiences that made miners build houses for their union officials so that they could not be ejected from colliery-owned homes, that made them build co-operative societies so that no future Lord Londonderry could frighten village shopkeepers into withholding credit from strikers, that for generations had left whole communities dependent for their existence on the will of some unknown, profit-hungry ' board of directors '—such experiences do not produce a far-sighted, moderate and benign attitude. The historical causes were clear, but the future effects ?

Chapter Six

THE PAST

JOHNSON had moved from the upstairs rooms in East Tanthope, beyond range of the suspicions of the ardent young Sam Forgan, as soon as possible. Fortunately he had been able to get a room in the house of an elderly widow on a council estate nearby. It had been difficult to explain the removal to the Kelso family, who seemed to suspect that he had been dissatisfied with the services they had provided ; and although he did his best, without divulging Sam Forgan's share in the affair, a slight sense of awkwardness persisted. If he called in on the Kelsos in the evening, the old lady behaved with a ceremony she had never shown while he had been a boarder. She would turn young Beryl out of the best armchair to give place to him, scold Connie for pouring his tea in a chipped cup, and by a hundred such little signs keep him at a respectful distance. Only old Tom, with a mind above domestic affairs, remained unchanged towards him. Johnson was still accorded, as of right, a chair at the table at the top end of the clubroom where Tom and the Lodge officials always sat : a privilege that carried very solid advantages with it, in the form of prompt service from the overworked barmen, and whisky and cigarettes, if required, even in times of acute shortage. On Sunday evenings, too, he was still invited to join the old man's whisky-drinking expedition to the city.

His room in the widow's house was not attractive, and whenever he had a couple of hours to spare in the evening Johnson would spend them in the Club, among the circle of elders. As he became more and more accepted, and perhaps even more as it became clear that he was acquiring a good working knowledge of the industry, he had to spend much less time listening to incoherent statements of the ' miner's case.' He was no longer regarded as a Southern gentleman to be won over before the coalowners got at him ; there were times, even, when they forgot he was a civil servant. But this did not mean that mining was not discussed. Indeed very little else was discussed. But now they talked to him of the hitch in the third Ballerat, of the number of tubs ' laid out ' that day, of the prices put in for the new bargain. Everyday, intimate pit-talk, that helped him to come close to their working life without an intervening fog of political prejudice and passion.

Their work obsessed them. They loved and hated it, were proud and ashamed of it, fascinated and repelled by it. They noticed their own confusion of feeling about it, and laughed helplessly. " They's more cowels won in t'Club than they is in t'pit," they would confess of their inability to leave work behind them at the end of the shift. And one man solemnly told Johnson that whenever he went to the local cinema he took good care to sit beside a woman —" if Ah sits next a man, he'll start tahkin' pitwark an' spoil t'show ! " Their knotted minds were the cockpits where contending forces wrestled—the social values of the day which gave prestige to clean hands and white collars, and respected a man for the quantities of goods he could consume ; and the biological values which find full and abiding satisfaction in the direct application of strength and skill to known and worthwhile ends. They were primary producers, fighting nature at its most unpredictable and uncontrollable to bring something useful from the depths to the surface of the earth. And in a world devoted to buying and possessing they had been made to feel somehow at fault. Yet when they could fend off for an hour or two the pressure of outside opinion, their talk became rich and heavy with some slow, deep comfort of the spirit.

More than most men, too, the miners Johnson talked with in the Club had a sense of the past. Their fathers and grandfathers had been miners, and had talked to them of their craft, as old Tom now talked with young Norman ; and out of the long evenings of pit talk reaching back through generations had developed something like a tribal memory. Indeed it was when they were recalling the past that you could most clearly distinguish the odd duality of their attitude to the pit. Old Tom, for instance, as a boy of ten had helped his father to collect straws from the fields in autumn, to be filled with gunpowder and used as cartridges to fire down the coal : in those days the hewer had had to fire the coal himself. He could remember, as his father sat at the cottage table plugging, filling and twisting the straws, his grandfather, still working about the pit in his eightieth year, speaking of how he himself, as a strapping youth, had been among the first to use explosives at the coal face, and of how frightened the older miners had been by the innovation. The night that old Tom had told this story, sitting at the clubroom table strewn with pint pots, the others had leaned forward eagerly to catch every word, and were soon adding their own stories. Dick Reay, the Lodge chairman, recalled how, as a stoneman opening a road through some old broken workings, he had come upon one of the old steel mills used

before the invention of the safety lamp to give light.   This
led to a story by someone else of hewers who breathed in
so much firedamp at the face that when they came home
and blew out the bedside candle their breath caught fire.
Tom Kelso was reminded of the wooden pick he had seen
in some colliery office or other, used in places where there
was so much firedamp that a spark from a steel pick would
cause an explosion.   Such a fund of stories might be
expected to lead straight to denunciations of the wicked
exploitations practised by the coalowners of those days :
in fact it led straight to a fierce argument as to exactly how
far inbye the workings had been carried in those days of
primitive ventilation, a severely technical argument, in
which the tales of several mining grandfathers were
evoked in evidence.   Discussion of the more general
political problems of the industry, Johnson noticed,
although pervaded with the same sense of continuity
between past and present, tended to draw upon a less
intimate, more stereotyped stock of stories.   Three or
four radical historians had written accounts of the pioneer
struggles of the trade unions in this county ; and the
union itself had issued cheap reprints of at least two of these
histories, which all the more serious-minded pitmen had
read.   These were full of lurid (though authentic) stories
of explosions and exploitations, strikes and lock-outs,
mass evictions, truck shops, hangings, jailings and trans-
portations.   These were not the stories that the miners,
in the relative prosperity of the later nineteenth century,
had passed on to their sons.   They had been forgotten,
and then deliberately revived, as political legendry, to
foster endurance and resolution in the sad inter-war years.

It was out of these yarnings round the table at the top
end of the clubroom that the idea of a local history research
group sprang.   That, too, was typical.   All these men had
a wistful respect for the ' scholard.'   They all had a vague
but strong feeling that if only miners as a body had been

better educated, as apt with fine words as their enemies, all their battles would now be won. Their union had been prolific in scholarships to Ruskin College, and although the results had bred disillusion in that particular institution (too many of the young men sent up to Oxford for a year to sharpen their wits had succeeded so well that they found jobs in other industries instead of returning to put their learning at the disposal of their mates), the local university, the W.E.A. and Labour College tutors all received ample support still. The presence among them of a sympathetic, university-trained mind revived all their latent regrets for misspent youth. There was a library room at the back of the Club, and the W.E.A. class would not be starting till October. Johnson was approached : would he lead a discussion group of some sort ?

The group started its weekly meetings with an attendance of a score of men, and for a month or so solemnly thrashed out its diverse opinions about the Government's coal policy, the recently issued White Papers on full employment and international finance and other such general issues. By the end of the month attendance was down to eight. These survivors, all intelligent men, all strongly endowed with an urge to self-education, were by this time much more specific about their needs. It wasn't just knowledge they wanted, but knowledge they could use. It was all very well debating the respective merits of the Bancor plan and the Unitas plan, but what could an East Tanthope miner do about it all when he'd made up his mind ? Brought thus sharply up against the central problem of democratic control, the group decided to restrict its enquiries to more local and manageable fields. It was Johnson who made the acceptable suggestion that they should investigate and write the history of the village.

It was gratifying how, once the news got around, the interest of the village was fired. The most astonishing historical material came to light : old newspaper cuttings and pamphlets, paintings, samplers, letters, clothes, pay-sheets. One miner produced a rule-card belonging to the first—short-lived—miners' union established in the coal-field; his great-grandfather had been a member. The local vicar produced a copy of the petition sent by the parishioners to Parliament to protest against the enclosing of the land on which the village now stood. One of the under-managers of the colliery asked if he could join the group, and as earnest of his good will brought along a number of early plans and account books from the colliery office archives. It became necessary to limit the size of the group to twelve members. One member, off for a few weeks because of an injury to his hand, got so interested that he spent four or five days a week in the Municipal Library in the city.

Almost too quickly the outlines of East Tanthope's growth began to emerge. It was a simple, and typical, history.

It began in 1773 when Sir John Elvet, M.P., a local landowner of considerable means, introduced a private Bill in the House of Commons for the enclosure of certain 'commonable lands,' estimated at 2,800 acres, in the neighbourhood of his estates. In spite of protests from the parishioners, an authorising Act was granted, and Sir John Elvet received a piece of pasture land of 900 acres as his share of the spoils.

In 1776 Sir John leased 300 acres of this land, a piece lying along the road from Tanthope Moor, to one Thomas Starr for arable farming. The lease retained for the landlord, due compensation to be made, rights of surface entry for the mining of minerals.

At this time the nearest colliery of any size was some six miles away, at Fair Fell on the other side of the Elvet estates. It was a pit belonging to the Grand Copartners, a partnership of three enterprising landowners who dominated the coal trade of the river. By a systematic leasing of royalties and wayleaves they had established a practical monopoly of the deeper, inland coal. Development of the coal on the Elvet estate was dependent on them for transport. The first sign of negotiations between Sir John Elvet and the Grand Copartners appeared in 1783, when the latter were granted the lease of royalties underlying part of the estate. A drift was sunk, and the wooden wagonway of the Copartners brought two miles nearer the farm at East Tanthope.

1784. Boring operations were carried out on a farm at East Tanthope.

1785. A shaft was sunk to a depth of 23 fathoms on the western edge of the farm holding. A row of twenty cottages was built nearby at a cost of £46 8s. 3d. each. The new pit was leased to a man called Bassett for £90 a year and certain additional payments on coals drawn above a certain amount.

1789. The workmen signing the annual bond with Bassett numbered twenty-two. (Together with their children, the actual number of people working at the pit would probably amount to sixty.) A second pit was sunk this year, and leased to Thomas Starr, the farmer.

Sir John Elvet died, and was succeeded by his son Charles.

1801. The population of the parish of Tanthope was returned as 273 (this includes a few mining families belonging to the Fair Fell pit). In the previous year, giving evidence to the Commission reporting on the Coal Trade, Sir Charles Elvet stated that he had sold corn and rye to the miners working on his estates at considerably below the market price, during the recent shortage. He had also, when speaking in the House of Commons during the debate on the Combination Bill, said that his pitmen earned three times as much as his farm labourers ; and " so little are the dangers of working in these pits, that in five years only two person have been killed, and one of these a lazy child that fell asleep and was trampled over in the dark."

1803. The Elvet account books shew that three pits,

two of them leased to 'Thomas Starr & Partner,' were now working at East Tanthope, and that the 'old pit' (presumably the first shaft sunk) had been closed. Ten more cottages, with gardens, and 'two good dwellings,' had been built. Permission is given to William Tranter, a pitman, to hold services and 'Sunday classes for the children' in a barn on the farm. Tranter, it seems, was a Primitive Methodist.

1805. A shaft of 32 fathoms was being sunk. At the annual bonding this year, fourteen guineas bounty-money was paid to the hewers, and eight guineas to the barrowmen, as compared with a guinea and half-a-guinea in 1789. More cottages were being built, and an ale-house.

1806. At the opening of the new pit a feast was given by Sir Charles Elvet's agent, a sheep being roasted whole and three barrels of beer consumed. A petition, signed by thirty pitmen headed by William Tranter, asks Sir Charles for a piece of land by the roadside on which to build themselves a chapel—"this village numbering 400 souls and hath no place for their Instruction." The petition was granted, and a piece of ground 'at the end of Old Row' specified for the purpose. The ale-house was leased to Thomas Starr.

1810. In October all the pitmen of the village, in concert with all miners in the coalfield, struck work against the demand of the colliery owners that the period of the current bond should be prolonged for a further three months. Starr, writing to Sir Charles Elvet in London, says that 'the ranting man Tranter' is laying the men under oath, and that several heads have been broken by the Militia at 'secret assemblings on the Moors.'

1811. On the bond signed in January of this year the signature of William Tranter does not appear, nor that of his son John.

1811–1820. Throughout these years mining operations at East Tanthope continued to be on a small scale—small pits working thirty or forty acres of top coal, then closing as other shafts were sunk. There never appears to be more than six pits working simultaneously. Why Sir Charles Elvet did not venture into the deep mining, that was proving so profitable elsewhere in the coalfield, is not quite clear. It is probable however that the Grand Copartners' virtual monopoly of transport facilities in this district imposed restrictions. It was the great period of the Vend, or combination of coalowners to restrict output, and the Grand Copartners dominated the combination.

1821. Population of village, 411.

In this same year, East Tanthope achieved the status of a civil parish, rated separately for the relief of its poor.

Following complaints by the vicar of the ecclesiastical parish, that his churchyard could not answer all the demands made on it by the new mining population, Sir Charles Elvet also provided the village with a consecrated burial ground of its own.

Starr, writing to Sir Charles Elvet, says that several of the pitmen " now call themselves Primitives, being a new sort of Ranting : and wear fine black suits o' Sunday."

The widow Sales with two children, a pauper, was boarded out in the workhouse of a neighbouring parish at a cost of 4s. 2d. a week. " Her cottage will stand empty for the bonding."

1823. An advertisement in the *County Mercury* invites gentlemen to purchase Twentieths in the new undertaking of Sir Charles Elvet & Partners to sink a new pit to the Main Coal at East Tanthope. Since this seam lies at a depth of 320 feet, this enterprise indicates that something has happened to ease the transport difficulties from the estate to the local distribution centres. And in fact the previous year an Act had been passed authorising the construction of one of the new railways from a point accessible to the estate to a port in the south of the county : the monopoly of the Grand Copartners was breaking down.

A surveyor's map of the village, dated this year, shows four rows of cottages—one on each side of the road running past the pits, with a shorter row running at right-angles at each end : perhaps eighty dwellings in all. The chapel, the cemetery, and ' Mr. Starr's shop & alehouse ' are also shown, with five other houses at intervals along the road.

An account of an auction, given in a local paper, suggests that the miners' cottages were well furnished, for a mahogany chair belonging to widow Walker was sold for £3 5s. Her husband, a barrowman, had been killed by a fall of stone some weeks earlier.

1825. Sinking is started on the shaft to the Main Coal. A speculative builder tendered for the building of forty new cottages in two rows at £32 apiece ; his tender was accepted. This contract was signed by Robert Starr— presumably the son of the old man.

1832. This same Robert Starr, writing to Sir Charles Elvet who had been in London for more than a year, supporting the Grey ministry through its difficulties, gives a survey of local conditions. There have been riots and steeks (strikes) since the bindings, led by some artful, infatuated rogues, he says ; but none of this trouble has yet reached East Tanthope. Nevertheless the pitmen talk much incendiary politics over their ale, and a number of men of late have protested saucily at the fines imposed in the pit. Since these were times of acute depression in the older part of the coalfield, it seems that the new pit is relatively prosperous. The population of the village is now 748.

1834. A new Boulton & Watt engine for winding coal was purchased for the new pit, now named the Mildred pit, after Sir Charles Elvet's granddaughter. Some more cottages are building—and a small row of ' double houses ' for minor officials of the pit. The new railways, with Stephenson's latest and at last successful locomotive running on them, had been spreading rapidly over the coalfield ;

and the duties on coal had been lowered. The newer pits—East Tanthope among them—were prosperous.

With the new winding engine came one of the new cages. The old corfs, or baskets, were discarded and small tubs running on iron rails were introduced in their place. This was the very latest thing in mining, and immediately produced a strike. After four weeks the candymen (bailiffs) were brought to the village and evictions began. A fortnight later the men resumed work on Sir Charles Elvet's terms.

In the late autumn an explosion occurred in one of the workings and six men and four lads were killed. The pitmen blamed the new tubs, saying that they interfered with the ventilation; Starr said that the tubs improved the ventilation (which was probably true) and that the pitmen were opposed to the new system only because it threw a number of the younger children out of employment (which was also probably true).

1841. Population: 1,017. For the greater part of this year the Mildred pit was working only three days a week. There are a great many complaints about the number of tubs 'laid out' for short measure and stopped from earnings: the men say that the new tubs, even though filled to the brim at the coal face, shake down to half the volume on these iron rails. Starr wrote an indignant letter to Sir Charles Elvet, warning him not to accede to a petition the pitmen are sending him, asking for a further piece of land to extend their chapel. Starr says there are agitators among the men, and they want the bigger chapel, not for worship, but for meetings.

1844. From April to July the Mildred pit—indeed most pits in the county—were laid idle by a general strike. In May evictions started, and a strange colony of blanket-bivouacs appeared on the moor a couple of miles from the colliery, while soldiers and a couple of hundred blacklegs, mostly Cornishmen, occupied the cottages. Starr, writing in answer to urgent enquiries from London, says that the situation is under control. " The deluded villains " have made no show of violence so far, but spend their time tramping away to meetings all over the county. They cannot last out much longer, he says. " Already they have to sell their homes where they stand in the fields. Daily they take away chairs, tables, even beds on a handcart to the city and exchange them for flour." For four months the pitmen stood out ; for more than two months they lived in their sad, strange encampment on the moors. At last, with all their possessions pawned or sold, with pit after pit starting up again and nothing gained, the men drifted back to the pithead, and the wives set up house again in the vacant cottages.

1845. Sir Charles Elvet built a school house in the village and appointed Samuel Fitt, a miner recently incapacitated in the pit, as schoolmaster. He also gave the pitmen permission to extend their chapel if they still desired to do so.

1847. Sinking began, on a piece of land a mile from the village, for the shaft of a new deep pit to the Hutton seam.

1848. After a series of minor misfortunes, the new shaft caved in at a depth of 420 feet, burying four men at work there. Sir Charles Elvet died at his London home, at the ripe old age of 92. The pitmen, in a memorial address, called him " a true Friend of enlightenment and the people," and said that 200 children were learning to read the word of God in the schoolhouse he had lately erected.

1849. The Alice pit, reaching the Hutton seam at a depth of 510 feet, was opened, and there were junketings in the village. The local newspaper expressed disappointment that on these occasions fewer and fewer pitmen sported the traditional garb of blue stockings, yellow breeks, white linen shirt and posy jacket : at East Tanthope, not more than a score of the oldest colliers were so attired.

In his will, the late Sir Charles Elvet had made a number

of bequests to the village: a sum of one hundred pounds for the improvement of the Methodist chapel, a piece of land and two thousand pounds for the building of a Church, and fifty pounds for a 'library of moral Books' to be attached to the school.

1851.   Population: 2,193.

1854.   Following an accident in the Mildred pit, a deputation of pitmen, including a representative of the minor officials, sought out Starr in his new offices in the city, and presented demands for (a) an increase in score prices, on the grounds that while the price per score of tubs had remained unchanged, larger tubs had been gradually introduced; and (b) systematic daily inspection of the workings.   Starr refused to treat with them, and warned the deputation that he would have " no new Unions among his men."

A new Starr is rising in the firmament of the Elvet undertaking—Edward, the son.   Now that his father is getting old, and is more and more concerned with the commercial side of affairs in the city, Edward is supervising production at the pits.   He is progressive, and has spent some time in ironworks.

A new terrace of cottages—in two parallel rows of forty— is in building.   Including these, the undertaking now owns about 400 cottages and dwellings in the village. There are, in addition, four beerhouses and three shops.

1856.   Edward Starr builds two coke-ovens, and revises the layout of the undertaking's surface transport system, purchasing two new engines and some new wagons.

1860.   Following the Mines Regulation Act of this year, the first miners' checkweighman was appointed by the pitmen: Jude Forgan.   For performing this duty he was paid 25/- a week from the Lodge funds.

1861.   Population: 3,927.   In May of this year Edward Starr married Alice, great-granddaughter of the late Sir Charles Elvet.   The pitmen presented them with a pair of thoroughbred hunters " as like as two peas "—which suggests, perhaps, that the romance bred in the counting-house was nourished on the sporting field.

1862. A branch of the Miners' Provident Association was formed at East Tanthope, following a terrible disaster at a pit some miles away where two hundred and fourteen men were buried alive. Edward Starr accepted the presidency of the branch, and Jude Forgan, hewer and lay preacher, was elected secretary. The object of the Association was to provide relief for the victims of mining accidents.

1863. Edward Starr resigned his presidency of the Provident Association branch on learning that Jude Forgan and other officials of the branch had, on Christmas Day of the previous year, attended an open-air meeting addressed by " notorious agitators " with the object of founding a new Union of Miners.

In March Jude Forgan led a deputation to Edward Starr to demand that various increases be made in the pit prices. To support the demands he produced the current paynotes of several of the best hewers, showing that not one of them was able to earn more than thirty-four shillings a fortnight. Starr countered this argument by alleging that the hewers were deliberately restricting their output. No agreement was reached.

In April, at a pithead meeting to sign the annual bond, Jude Forgan refused his signature and the rest of the men followed him. Edward Starr, addressing the men, announced that in the course of the year two new seams were to be opened in the Alice pit, and the Mildred shaft was to be sunk to a lower seam—all of which would allow the men to earn ample money at the present prices. After some deliberation by the men, the bond was signed.

1866. A deputation to Edward Starr, again led by Jude Forgan, complained about the sanitation of the older cottages in the village, saying that they had no privies, and that water had to be brought, in some cases, from a

distance of two hundred yards.   The men ask that a privy
be provided for each two cottages, and a water tap for
each four cottages, to bring all the cottages in the village
up to the standard of the new ones in Elvet Terrace.   Starr
replied he had had some such improvements under consideration for some time, and would do what he could.

1867.   A wage advance was agreed upon.

The ' Provident ' branch funds showed a balance of £300
this year.   In the five years of its existence, four grants of
ten pounds each had been made to widows of men killed
in the pits, and more than £400 had been paid out in weekly
grants varying from half-a-crown to ten shillings to men
laid idle by accidents.

1870.   Jude Forgan and James Dale were given notice
to leave the pit because of their activities on behalf of the
new miners' union, founded in the previous year.   The
two men wrote a joint letter to the county newspaper,
protesting against this victimisation, and stating that
employers should welcome this new method of settling
disputes amicably, instead of by violence.

To this move the pitmen replied by forming a co-operative
society among themselves, and paying Dale a small salary
to manage it.   They also voted a small salary to be paid to
Forgan as secretary of the ' provident.'   A Lodge of the
new union was formed in the village, with a foundation
membership of sixteen : Forgan and Dale were elected
Secretary and Chairman respectively.   One of the first
acts of the new Lodge was to invite the women of the
village to make a broad banner of blue velvet, on which
was to be embroidered in gold the device of a fraternal
handshake against a rising sun, and beneath it the legend :
OUT OF THE NIGHT OF HATE, THE DAWN OF
LOVE.

1871.   Population : 5,119.

The new co-operative society was so successful under
Dale's management that two of the shops in the village,

owned by overmen, were closed ; and the society took over one of the vacated premises. Membership of the union rose to 382. In this year old Robert Starr died, and was reputed to have left his son more than two hundred thousand pounds.

An explosion in the Hutton seam at the Alice pit killed seven men and two horses. (Oddly enough, although horses must have been introduced into the East Tanthope pits much earlier, this is the first mention of them in the records.)

1872. Jude Forgan was re-employed at the Alice pit, and Starr's new viewer formally accepted the principle of negotiation by and through the elected officials of the Lodge.

1873. The Company requested the assistance of the Lodge in checking the growing abuses to its property due to the keeping of pigeons and dogs by the pitmen.

1874. The pit stood idle for a week owing to a strike against reduced wages. The agents of the union having accepted the reduction, the men were finally persuaded to return to work ; and the Company thanked the Lodge for its efforts in the matter.

1877. This was a black year for the village. In March wages fell again for the third time in three years. A co-operative colliery, in which Lodge funds and the private savings of many of the men had been invested, closed down in bankruptcy. The pits were working only two or three days a week. Membership of the union dropped from 1,100 to 600. Several young men from the village were driven to emigrate to America. In June the Lodge recorded a somewhat bitter vote of thanks to the vicar of St. Dunelm's (the new church) for " the bread of charity he has given this week to our children." At the end of the year, and for the greater part of the following year, the working of two seams was suspended in the Alice pit and one seam in the Mildred pit, leaving four hundred men wholly unemployed. The village co-op., although it allowed credit to only the most desperate cases, had to cease giving credit altogether when it found the village owed it £2,000.

1879. At the beginning of the year the coalowners of the county stated that the men must accept an immediate wage-cut of 20 per cent., and refused to put the issue to arbitration. In March a general strike was called, and it was July before a settlement was reached—the case going at last to arbitration and a reduction of only 10 per cent. awarded. This five months' ordeal, following the rigours of the previous two years, left the villagers with little to rely on save the produce of their gardens. The vicar assumed the proportions of a saint during these months. In April he began to give the schoolchildren a slice of bread in their classroom. Within a week attendance at the school increased fourfold, sturdy lads of fifteen and sixteen wanting to have lessons. By appeals to friends in the south he contrived, not only to feed his strange multitude, but by pressing his wife and daughter into service, educate them as well. Before the strike ended, the membership of the Lodge had risen again to 1,100.

1881. Population: 5,733. A branch of the County Franchise Association was formed in the village, with the object of removing the legal anomaly which disallowed the vote to pitmen living in 'free' houses. Prosperity was returning to the village; the new Bessemer steel process had given a fillip to the iron foundries, and these to the coal trade. The suspended workings were opened again in both pits. The indebtedness of the village to the co-op. stores was being gradually reduced.

1882. In January, on a snowy day, a cart came into the village preceded by a man with a wooden rattle. He was collecting bread for the strikers of a colliery some ten miles away. When the cart left the village it was piled high with loaves.

1885. The undertaking was reconstituted as a limited liability company, Elvet & Starr, Ltd., and there was a small public issue of shares. Soon afterwards, the company bought the Fair Fell pit, on the other side of the Elvet royalties. The galleries of the Alice and Mildred pits had long been linked at the Main Coal level : the two pits were now merged, using the Mildred shaft for riding and the Alice for coal drawing. Soon after the pit was re-opened, there was a strike of putters, who claimed that the re-organisation of the underground transport had made their work more difficult, and that an increase in their prices was warranted. Jude Forgan persuaded the young men to return to work.

It was the veteran unionist's last success. A few weeks later he died at the age of 67, and with the company's consent the pit was closed for a day that the men might follow him to his grave.

1887. Subscriptions were raised among the pitmen for the foundation of a Workmen's Social Club. A piece of land was bought, and a club-house built, 1,400 members having bought one-pound shares in the venture.

1888. The pitmen voted for the first time in a local government election, and had the satisfaction of seeing a miners' representative returned to the County Council.

1891. Population : 6,254.

1892. A demand by the coalowners for a reduction of 13½ per cent. in the wage rates was resisted by a strike of the whole county ; the strike lasted twelve weeks. The severity of this blow on the life of the village was sharpened by the fact that, for the first time, enginemen and deputies struck too, so that no maintenance work was done while the pit lay idle. The distress was such that men were thought to be eating their dogs : certainly all the pigeons that could not be sold went into the stockpots. Strike pay amounted only to 25/- per head for the whole period. Although the strike ended in June, work could not be

recommenced immediately, for the roads in the pit had
fallen in at several places, and two working districts were
flooded. Lotteries were held weekly to decide which
men should be re-employed, not more than one man from
each family being eligible in the first weeks. Even so it
was weeks before men were fit enough to do a normal day's
work. By October the pit was shipshape again, but not so
the markets ; throughout the winter the men were working
only four days a week.

1895. Three officials of the Lodge were elected to the
newly established parish council. One of these, the
secretary, Andrew Reay, was also elected to the Rural
District Council, which in this year had a majority of
miners' representatives.

1897. Two blocks of very old cottages were pulled
down, and improvements made in the cottages of Elvet
Terrace.

1901. Population : 6,152.

1904. A three-day strike at the colliery, due to dissatisfaction with the prices paid for work with some coal-
cutting machines recently introduced, was settled by
arbitration.

1907. A row of six two-roomed cottages, with front
and back gardens, for the use of aged miners, was built
with money raised in equal proportions by the union and
the owners.

1908. The Workmen's Social Club was extended,
and a library for the use of its members added.

1912. A general strike being ordered by the Mineworkers' Federation at the beginning of March, for the
purpose of obtaining a national minimum wage, the East
Tanthope pit was laid idle for five weeks. This was the
first time the pitmen of East Tanthope had been involved
in a struggle the origins of which lay outside the county
(the trouble had started in South Wales) ; and there was
little enthusiasm for the strike among the older pitmen.

Government intervention secured the main principle of the miners' demands.

1914. On August 10th, news of Lord Kitchener's appeal for a hundred thousand men reached the village : on the same day 193 pitmen walked to the county town and took the King's shilling.

Only a few weeks before this event, Lord Elvet, chairman of Elvet & Starr, Ltd., addressed the annual meeting of shareholders. After giving production figures for the past thirty years, he went on : " You will notice that wages have risen from 25/3 in 1893 to 34/9 in 1913—that is, upwards of 35 per cent. . . . In 1893 the country was about to embark on a process of so-called social reform, and the tale of our working costs since then is briefly the tale of legislation, not in the interests of the community generally, but of individuals in your employment. Since the Workman's Compensation Act, we have had to pay more than £65,000 in compensation. Workman's Insurance, a comparatively recent piece of legislation, has already cost us more than £3,000. The Eight Hours Act, passed against the best judgment of both miners and mine-owners in this county, has cost us £45,000. Last year alone the Rescue and Aid Act cost us £300, the Coal Mines Act cost us £7,500, the Minimum Wage Act cost us £3,000. Add to all this an annual increase in the local rates amounting to £10,000, and you find that more than £41,000 has been added to the annual cost of production."

The company declared a dividend on ordinary stock of 7½ per cent. for the year.

1916. The son of the Lodge Chairman resisted conscription on the grounds of conscientious objection, and was sent to prison. There was a one-day sympathetic strike on the part of the putters, of whom he was the acknowledged leader. In this and the following year there was a good deal of dissatisfaction, leading to sporadic strike action by sections of the men, due to the adoption of the longwall method of working, with face-conveyors, to replace the traditional bord-and-pillar method of working.

1919. A memorial was erected to the forty-seven men of the village who had been killed in action.

A branch of the Labour Party was formed, and grew rapidly to a membership of 500.

A cinema was opened. Three months after it started business, the proprietor posted a notice announcing that he was no longer prepared to give credit.

1920. There was a one-week strike for increased wage rates.

1921. On March 31st the Government relinquished its control of the coal mines: on April 1st a national strike began. The East Tanthope pit was closed for three months; but there was comparatively little distress in the village. Union funds were plentiful, the weather was good, and in June it was possible for the Lodge to send some of the village children to the seaside for an afternoon.

1925–1926. The village followed the negotiations between the Government and the T.U.C. with breathless interest; during April several labour speakers addressed meetings, the attendance at Lodge meetings was unparalleled, and delegates were sent off to several demonstrations. During the last days of April a notice appeared at the pithead announcing that the existing terms and conditions of employment would terminate on May 1st: the new rates would mean a reduction of current wages by 27 per cent., and an eight-hour shift instead of seven-and-a-half. No one turned up for work on May 1st—men, women and children were at a tremendous May Day demonstration in the county town. It was seven months before the East Tanthope pit opened again.

During the first fortnight the village was bewildered: this was not like any other strike they had known. While the pitmen were locked out, the rest of the country was in the throes of the General Strike. The Government was behaving as though it had a civil war on its hands. There were rumours of riots, police charges, shootings. The arrest of one of their own county agents seemed to lend credence to the rumours. News, such as there was, came to them in odd little mimeographed sheets. Parties of men walked into the city to find out what was going on, and came back with stories of special constables patrolling in twos and a terrible shortage of beer. Some of the youngsters set up something they called a Council of Action, with a sense of revolution in the air, and began issuing a mimeographed sheet of their own. All over the county there were demonstrations, open-air meetings, conferences: attending them gave the men something to do. Then came the news that the General Council of the T.U.C. had called off the General Strike. It was a bitter blow, but in a way a relief: the village could settle down again to the kind of strike it was used to. The co-op. decided to allow its members a credit of five pounds per head. The Board of Guardians was granting relief at the normal scales. There was a small issue of strike pay, and, as the lock-out went into its second and third month, money from various funds came into the village to buy shoes and clothes and school meals for the children. The weather was excellent, the allotments doing well. There were cricket matches. . . .

But slowly the familiar features of despair settled over the village. There were gaps in every home where the hire-purchase people had taken back their furniture, or in-essentials had been sold. Little bands of young men decided to try their luck at tramping. A cigarette would be shared between four or five men, each taking a couple of draws and passing it on.

As winter came on it became evident that the struggle was lost. In November, while the County Association was still negotiating with the owners, making a last desperate effort to secure some small modification of the terms, the Lodge withdrew its pickets from the pit gates. The fight that had cost the country £350,000,000 was over. The village, gaunt and threadbare, owing a debt of £23,000 for co-op. credits and poor relief, with its wages reduced by 27 per cent., went back to work.

1928.   The steady demand for coal in the year following the lock-out began to ease up, and the effects of the lost export markets were felt: a number of the older men were given their cards, the pit closed for three weeks in the summer, and through the autumn it worked three or four days a week only.   Percentage unemployment for the year: 10·1.

1929.   Percentage unemployment: 9·7.

1930.   Percentage unemployment: 17·8.

1931.   Population of the civil parish of East Tanthope: 7,093.   Percentage unemployment of insured workers: 22·4.

1932.   Percentage unemployment: 30·1.

1933.   Percentage unemployment: 29·8.

1934.   Percentage unemployment: 25·5.

In this year the Rural District Council, with assistance from the County Council, acquired 110 acres of land at the northern end of the village and began the building of a model housing estate.   A number of pitmen were employed on the work.

1935.   Percentage unemployment: 19·7.

1936.   In this year a Welfare Institute, with tennis courts and bowling green, was built by the Miners' Welfare Commission.

Percentage unemployment: 16·8.

1937.   Percentage unemployment: 17·1.

1938.   Percentage unemployment: 14·3.

1939.   Percentage unemployment: 10·4.   Stimulated by an increase in the number of men employed and by improved earnings over the past two years, it was decided to rebuild and enlarge the Workmen's Club.

Building was also started on a canteen and pithead bathhouse, funds being provided by the Miners' Welfare Commission.

Such were the simple annals of East Tanthope, this village that had lived by digging holes in the ground. As the holes grew bigger and deeper, the village had grown with them. For a century and a half the pit had dominated its life, shaping the people to suit its purposes, killing and maiming them, giving a proud prosperity and snatching it back, throwing up a grey rampart of slag to isolate the village from the world, binding it in fierce exiguous loyalties. Arbitrary and unaccountable its behaviour, to the men who were dragged from its galleries burnt or mangled, to the women who tried to keep homes clean and tables laden with the wages it paid. Yet to those who had endurance and hardihood enough to survive its ways, it gave a deep sombre pride and satisfaction. Nothing had come easily to this village. When it felt a need, it had tried to supply it for itself, and if anyone opposed the effort, the village had fought. Every institution in the village with the exception of the cinema, the post-office and the church, the people had built themselves or struggled for through their union. Their community, forged deep underground in dark stony places, drew on elemental sources of strength and discipline. Personal ambition was tamed to the Lodge office, the committee table, the pulpit and the craft of the pit. The customs of the community, both underground and on the surface, were old and honoured for their age ; the double isolation of craft and geography had turned these people in upon themselves, so that they took their standards from their forebears instead of from the strangers in the city. Often they resisted change to their detriment. The working customs of the pit—the cavil, the bargain, the stint, the complicated piece-rate payments, the hundred separate little agreements about picks and lamps and what-have-you—these were survivals of an era of plenty that tended to become fetters in time of dearth. But their history was important to them. Its victories were the worn paths of their living; its defeats were the marrow in their bones. This was the deeper sense that glowed through all the contradictions of those men in the Club— their pride and humility, their silences and violences, their innocence and guile : so far their history had brought them, so much had it achieved—why then take all these propagandists and alarmists seriously ?—they were strong, patient and daring, their history would take them farther still.

Chapter Seven

THE OWNER

THE arrival of the cinema apparatus coincided with one of Major Salter's rare visits to the regional offices. Johnson had rigged the projector up in his room, and was running through a short technical film to a mixed audience of labour officers and girls from the typists' pool when the Major came in.

" I say, Tom, we'll have to. . . . "

He was going to say ' prosecute,' but then he took in the pallid gloom of the room and the bright little rectangle of light with its animated shadows. " Films, dammit ! " he said instead. By the time the reel was run through he had forgotten his original mission.

" Just the thing for my club ! " he enthused. " Lads'll love it . . . sixteen, seventeen year olds, you know. Always wanted a gadget like that for 'em—keep 'em away from the damn cinemas, it will ! "

He fussed around, inspecting the projector, the portable screen, the tangle of cables writhing across the floor.

" What's this ? And that ? " he demanded. " Speaks too, does it ? . . . 'Mazing, the things they get up to these days ! Have to show me how to work it, can't let the lads handle a thing like this, must cost a mint of money ! Easy to cart around, too, eh ? Just what I've been looking for ! "

Johnson began to feel alarmed. He hastened to explain that the projector had been sent down from headquarters to give showings of technical films to pit production committees. But the Major interrupted him.

" Technical films ? My dear boy, can't give that sort of stuff to these lads ! Cowboys, Charlie Chaplin, rattling good sea yarns, that's what they want ! "

" I've no doubt," Johnson said a trifle impatiently. " But the Ministry hasn't got around to supplying that sort of film yet. And I'm expected to keep the projector going full time round the collieries."

But to Major Salter such talk was meaningless. " Pits are too busy to waste their time with that sort of thing— or if they aren't they oughter be ! Much better get some good films and show 'em to my lads . . . where they'll be 'preciated, don't you know ? " The Major was nearly seventy. Films were a menace or they were a toy : that they were also a means of spreading new technical knowledge and ideas could never occur to him. Johnson saw that his inexplicable refusal to hand over three hundred pounds, worth of Ministry property for the exclusive use of the Cannockdene Boys' Club was beginning to irritate the Major, and since he had no wish to frustrate a laudable impulse he suggested a compromise. If the Major would organise a Film Club among his boys, and the club would meet the expenses of hiring the films it wanted to see, then Johnson would bring the equipment over once a month and give a show. The Major obviously did not think highly of the idea, but when he found these were the only terms on which he could obtain the use of the projector for his club he agreed. Johnson was invited to come over to dinner with him the following Sunday, and then go along to the club with him later and put the scheme up to the boys.

It was the first time Johnson had had a chance to talk with one of the possessing class of the coalfield. It is true that in the hierarchy of coal ownership Major Salter was fairly small beer. He had been transferred to the Ministry at the salary he had received from his company— fifteen hundred a year—but his holdings in the company were probably small, and his directorship had been an award for good service. Of the great coal barons of the county, a few still remained on visiting terms with their local estates, but the centres of their interests had now passed elsewhere. The old Major was as big a wig as was likely to be found within the vicinity of a colliery.

The dinner was good, and amusing after the inevitable apologies had been got through—Johnson having to excuse himself for not having a dress suit with him, Mrs. Salter having to claim indulgence for the new and hesitant maid, the Major himself asking that his wife be allowed to sit through the port. After some preliminary skirmishing round the subjects of golf and rough shooting, the con- versation settled down to London tailoring and restaurants : and it was only after half an hour of these gruelling social tests that Johnson knew he was considered acceptable. The Major laid down his cigar and stood up.

" If we go over to the club now," he said invitingly, " we can get back early and settle down to a good jaw. I've still got some real whisky left."

The club was only ten minutes away, and three of those were taken with getting out of the grounds. To a fidgeting audience of boys with brilliant ties jutting out of their Sunday suits Johnson put his proposition. (Can they still smell our cigar-reek ? he wondered.) How many times a week did the village cinema change its programmes, he asked? Twice, he was told. He started talking about the economics of the bi-weekly programme, explaining that the people who now owned most of the cinemas also made most of the films. That meant they wouldn't show films made by other people. It also meant they had to make enough films to keep their cinemas fairly full. If they could get people into the fixed habit of going to the cinema twice a week whatever was showing, what would happen? They would make cheaper and cheaper films, not worrying about quality but only cost, and the public would get less and less value for its money. The only way to get good films was to learn what made a film good, and then demand it loudly—and stay away from the cinema until it was provided. Or better still, run your own cinema! Supposing a club like this had its own projector—then at a charge of threepence a head it could hire films for itself, choosing its own programmes. . . .

" What about Russian films, mister? " one of the boys asked challengingly. (They *can* smell the cigar-reek, thought Johnson.)

" Certainly Russian films, if you want them."

" But we haven't got a projector."

When Johnson told them that he could provide the projector if they were prepared to hire the films, the whole scheme caught. He left the boys haggling about how to run the new Film Club. As they walked back towards the real whisky the Major congratulated him. " Must say though," he said, " didn't know the damn film business was that complicated! Always thought there was something fishy in it—all those damn leg-shows they make. Of course we'll have to knock all that talk about Bolshie films on the head—anyway, they don't make films, do they? "

" They've made some very good ones," Johnson said.

The Major pondered this information. " Can't say I've seen any," he said suspiciously.

The whisky *was* good. Johnson asked the Major about the club. The old man was pathetically proud of it. "My idea, my idea entirely," he said vaingloriously. "Company was getting a bit worried, all the youngsters getting jobs in the city. This was back in '37 and '38, mind you, when the trade was picking up a bit. Way it looked, there wouldn't be a boy working in the pit inside ten years. So I thought, must do something to make the village more attractive to the youngsters. Well, there was that old shed there—company didn't want it now. Quite big enough, I thought, but it'll take a bit of money to tidy it up. Well, there I was talking about it in the club one day, and a fella tells me about this George Fifth Fund. Just the very thing! So I got busy, and they gave us a grant."

Ethical problem : should public subscription funds be used to solve the labour problems of an individual colliery ? Johnson decided not to pursue the point, but asked instead, "And are the lads taking to the pit more readily now ? "

The Major shook his head, a lean, snowy, handsome head. No, he admitted, they weren't. They could earn more money in the factories round the city, and the fathers encouraged them to do so. They'd travel twenty miles, some of these lads, rather than work in the pit on their doorstep.

"And the few we do get—scum of the earth, some of 'em. Cheeky, undisciplined hooligans! Won't join the club, won't play any games. Put 'em underground, they're always last to ride, and spend their time derailing tubs and cutting telephone wires instead of working. Week-ends they go around in gangs insulting girls, breaking down walls, uprooting railings and being as destructive as they can! It's scandalous. D'you know what a gang of 'em did last week ? Put grease on the brake-handles of all the trucks in the sidings, hoping there'd be an accident! I'm an old man, and I've never seen anything like it before!

Something'll have to be done about it before it gets any worse ! "

So moved was the Major by the picture he had painted that his beautifully courtly manners forsook him and he stood and shouted.

" What do you think ought to be done ? " Johnson asked.

The Major sat down again, shaking his head. " It's beyond me," he confessed. " People like me, we've got no influence any more. Speak to their fathers ? That doesn't do any good nowadays. And it's worse since the war—can't sack 'em, they can laugh in your face, and they do ! Too much money, too many cinemas, too much drink, too many buses to take 'em to the city ! "

" Can't you do something drastic, like sack the fathers if the sons don't behave themselves ? " Johnson said solemnly. But the Major shook his head.

" That was all right when work was short. But they weren't like that then, we didn't have to pay 'em the money. I tell you, we got our hands tied by this damn Work Order. We can't do anything. It's up to your Ministry to make an example of a few of 'em ! "

Johnson coughed timidly. " You know, Major, you're quite an important person in the Ministry yourself. It's much more your Ministry than mine. Why don't you suggest something ? "

" Suggest ? My dear boy, I'm always suggesting. No idea of the amount of work I do, going through all the absentee reports to pick out the really bad eggs and recommend prosecution ! And what happens ? " He glanced across at his wife, knitting placidly by the window. " Nothing," he substituted. " Nothing at all."

Walking home after that conversation (for the Major's house was only a matter of four miles from East Tanthope), Johnson found himself trying to see the industry through the Major's eyes. I and my kind, the old man would doubtless say, have in a hundred and fifty years built a great industry. We put everything we had into it—money, brains, initiative. By doing so we raised England from a rut of history to become the proudest power of the world. The destiny of England, as Professor Tyndall pointed out in its heyday, was not in the hands of its statesmen but in those of its coalowners. Was the reward we got too great for so great an achievement? Cheap coal was the basis of the nation's prosperity; and we have fought tooth and nail against everything that might raise the price of coal. But now the prosperity we created returns to plague us. The easy living we gave to others has at last infected our workmen: workmen we had bred in the pride of the pit, schooled to hazard, seasoned to the dark elements. With them in the old days we had struggles, and the strongest won: but always the country got the cheap coal it needed. But now the friends of soft living—the soft living we created—fight with the workmen and not with us. Every victory they gain over us sends up the price of coal. Compensation Acts, Hours of Work, Wage Increases, Essential Work Orders. Then finding that their prosperity wanes as coal costs go up, they tell us we are inefficient. They shackle us with their statutes and controls, and tell us we are inefficient! We—who invented railways as a mere by-product of our needs! We—who have held back flood and fire in the bowels of the earth! They would send us their stop-watch engineers from London to shew us how to run our mines, they would send us their pansy social workers to teach us how to handle our labour! They would do everything except the one thing we want them to do—leave us alone so that we can solve the problems they have created without interference!

It was a viewpoint as hereditary and inevitable as the miner's own, instinct with pride and authority. With truth enough, too, to pronounce the terms of its own indictment. For the coalowners had themselves been among the first to succumb to the facile prosperity they had

I

created. They had discovered 'responsibilities' which required them to live in London and spend the autumn in Scotland. They had discovered the many advantages of investing the money they made from coal in the industries that used the coal. They had spent so much time dog-matising in Westminster of the immutable laws of economics that they had no time to observe the local workings of those laws in East Tanthope. Instead they left Major Salter behind to observe for them—a sound, stout fellow, known to have the right opinions on these matters.

Poor Major Salter! The house he lived in was the one old Robert Starr had built for himself while still engaged in the active direction of his pits. (But the Starrs had long since bought an estate in the south of the county, beyond the hideous pit villages, and a town house in Cadogan Square.) He could live a quiet, gentlemanly life there, proud of his Sheraton dining suite and his wine cellar, going up to London twice a year to order a suit and put in an appearance at his club, reading the lessons in the parish church and giving a garden party for the village children in the summer—but he could not direct the destiny of the coal trade. The three villages that lay under his super-vision as chief agent of Elvet & Starr Ltd. had between them the population of a fair-sized town and the social resources of a small hamlet. Of the eleven hundred houses owned by the company, there was not one that would satisfy the normal requirements of the average London factory worker. From these three villages, during the depression years, more than five hundred young men had migrated to other parts of the country, and had written home telling of what they had seen. Those migrants had been the best of their generation; the young men who remained behind, during years when the pit wanted them for only a day or two a week at most, had built new social habits around the impulses of boredom and resent-ment : habits which they had passed on to the boys of the generation following them, habits which made them unfitted for the responsibilities and disciplines of pitwork, and uninterested in the whole process of wage earning. What could poor Major Salter be expected to do about it? All his life there had been boys waiting at the pit head for employment, only too willing to work. How could he be expected to foresee a day when he could only employ them on their own terms? His club came too late. If Robert Starr or his Elvet partner, or even their children, had had thought for the social amenities of the villages they created, things might have been different.

Yet for all that Major Salter took his boys' club very seriously. So much so that within the week he was in Johnson's office again seeking information about the hiring of films. The boys had decided, he said, that they wanted to see a Russian film first.

" Damn difficult, if you see what I mean. Can't start this thing off by showing Bolshie propaganda, can I? Yet if I don't, they'll throw the whole thing overboard. What's your view, eh? You know more about it than I do."

" Don't worry," Johnson assured him. " The boys won't understand a word of it. And we'll throw in a couple of our own propaganda shorts just to make sure they don't get any wrong ideas."

So Johnson wrote off to the British Film Library for a copy of *The Road to Life*, and went round to the Ministry of Information to rout out a couple of the Government's more incendiary documentaries. On the following Friday evening, immediately after work, he drove out to Cannock-dene with the equipment and set it up in the club's gymnasium.

It was then that he learnt there were to be distinguished people present in the audience. Mrs. Salter arrived, with a gardener bearing some canvas chairs, to announce that there had been a board meeting that afternoon, and a couple of the directors were staying with the Major overnight and wanted to see the show.   She had ordered dinner late, and would Johnson stay for food when the films were through ?

Ten minutes later the boys began to arrive, most wearing chokers and their second-best suits for the occasion.   A few had brought their girls with them, and one or two, after a word with the club-leader, brought in their parents. Two or three officials of the local Lodge came in when the hall was nearly full, and took seats on a form at the back of the hall.   There was much excited staring and whispering as Johnson switched on the projector and fiddled with the focus.   He made the job last as long as possible, since there was no sign yet of the Major and his guests, although it was a quarter of an hour since Mrs. Salter went back to fetch them.   The young men on their wooden forms grew restive and started clowning among themselves, with an eye on the girls.   The Lodge secretary came over and asked questions about the equipment. When the Major and his guests arrived at last, the audience had been waiting for twenty minutes.   Mrs. Salter and the two men took their seats in the canvas chairs put out for them ; the Major stood in front of the screen to speak.

" Ah, happy to see so many familiar faces here to-night," he said, throwing his silvery head up with a jerk at every third or fourth word.   " Ah, don't have to tell you what it's all about.   Chose the film yourself, you did, and we've done our best to oblige.   Can't say I think much of your choice, but we won't go into that, eh ? Ha, ha. It's a free country, and if you want to see Bolshie films, well, let's get on with it."

There was some polite clapping, and someone put the lights out.   As Johnson switched on the projector, and a blare of militant music came from the loud speaker, the Major stumbled through the beam along the central aisle, a fandango of bright shadows dancing over his embarrassed features.   Then the screen was full of ragged urchins, and one of them, more noble-looking than the rest, grew impassioned about something. They took to digging, laying railway tracks, wiping sweat from their brow. A villainous looking man scowled. Streamers, flowers and banners decorated a railway platform. The villainous looking man killed the noble looking lad. The other lads found the body ; a train entered the screen ; the body was reverently placed on the cowcatcher of the engine. A crowd looked on mournfully as the train, with the body on the cowcatcher, drew to a halt at the gaily decorated station. Escaping steam gave out long dying sighs.

The boys were obviously disappointed with the film. Not so the Major. " See the idea ? " he said loudly and enthusiastically. " Hard work, build things, railways, mines, don't hang round street corners getting up to mischief ! "

Johnson put another spool on the projector. " This next picture," he told the audience, " is a short English film."

It was a film about the shipyards along the river : everybody in the audience recognised the place immediately. It showed the shipyards in the depression, high with weeds, the slipways rotted, the buildings fallen in. Then it showed the place being built up again in wartime, and the difficulties of persuading the old skilled workers, now dispersed in a hundred different occupations, to come back to the trade that had given them such bitter dealings. So few of them could be found, and there were so many ships to build, that girls had to be trained to do the jobs. Then, as a proud ship went down the slipway to the swelling chorus of a local song, a grim-voiced worker turned to the camera and asked : " Yes, you want us and our ships now there's a war on—but what about after the war, will the weeds come back and the slipways rot again ? "

That the boys did like. It was a film about the things they knew presented in the terms they thought of them. As Johnson began to collect his spools the club-leader stood up and thanked him on their behalf, and they clapped and went out humming the song they had just heard over the loudspeaker. The Major came over to the projector, turkey-red.

" That last film, did you say it was made by the Government ? "

" Ministry of Information," Johnson said. " They've done dozens like it, for showing in factory canteens, you know."

" Scandalous ! Can't believe it ! It's . . . it's . . . *asking* for trouble. Don't you agree, Starr ? " He became mild again as he effected introductions. " By the way, this is Mr. Starr, our chairman of directors. Mr. Johnson of the Ministry."

" More bolshie than the bolshie himself ! " Mr. Starr said warmly as he shook hands. He was a small, wizened man with heavy lidded eyes that gave him a reptilian appearance. The tall spruce man behind was introduced as a Sir William Dinton. " Now what good d'you think you do making pictures like that, I'd like to know ? " Starr demanded.

As they walked across to the house Johnson tried to explain that he was not responsible for the Ministry of Information's film policy. It was not easy, for civil servants were obviously lumped together in Mr. Starr's mind as an indistinguishably satanic crowd. No sooner had Johnson succeeded in dissociating himself from the evils of one group of bureaucrats than he found himself saddled with those of another group.

" Oh, you're in the Coal Control, are you ? Then you tell this fellow Gowers from me. . . ."

" Gowers ? " Johnson asked timidly.

" The Coal Controller."

" Commissioner," Johnson corrected as light came to him.

" Controller, commissioner, it's all one. Just had a letter from him up at the board to-day. Amalgamation, if you please ! He wants us. . . ."

Arrival at the house put a temporary halt to his grievances, but both he and Dinton returned to the subject over dinner. It seemed that that august body, the Coal Commission, having nearly completed its task of acquiring and unifying the coal royalties of the country, had now turned to the second part of its statutory duties. Parliament had entrusted to the Commission the duty of furthering the amalgamation of the multitudinous undertakings which worked the nation's coal. Now the Commission had circulated a letter to the colliery companies, reminding them of this duty, and asking them to submit proposals.

" What's he expect us to do, this Gowers ? Can't expect us to take over pits that can't pay for themselves and never will ! "

A picture of the royalty-map of the coalfield came into Johnson's mind, with its seventy or eighty irregular-shaped little patches. Where the boundaries of these patches joined, barriers of coal, forty yards thick, had to be left. In this coalfield alone, more than 250 million tons were sterilised in this way—more than the annual yield of the entire industry.

" The general idea," said Johnson, " is that amalgamations might enable some of the pits to pay for themselves, that can't do so at present."

" General idea ! " said Mr. Starr vehemently. " That's theory, but let's get down to fact ! "

" Of course, in your case I don't know all the facts off-hand," Johnson had to admit. " But I believe your royalties touch those of seven or eight other companies at different points. Let's say eight undertakings within a radius of five miles of this place. Each with its own power plant, supply stores, repair shops, pumping plant. Each having to leave large areas of coal unworked in the boundaries. Each in normal times maintaining its own pool of unemployment. None of you with adequate training facilities, or cleaning plant, or housing accommodation, or overground transport. Above all, none of you with the capital resources to remedy these shortcomings. That's the sort of. . . ."

But Mr. Starr and his co-directors could remain silent no longer. With antiphonic effect, they blurted out their indignation.

" We can produce coal as cheaply as anyone in this coal-field."

" We get a small enough return on our capital as it is, why should we put in more ? "

" Prove that a big organisation is more efficient than a small one ! "

" We've got the best equipment for miles round here."

Johnson had not the kind of courage that is prepared to take on three aggressive men on their own ground and terms. He shrugged. " I don't know enough about these things to argue with you. All I've said is what three successive Royal Commissions have said about the industry. What Parliament itself said, when it set up the Coal Commission to deal with these matters." There was good partridge on his plate, and a pleasantly acid red wine in his glass ; he had no wish to embarrass his host.

Mr. Starr relaxed. " Oh, Royal Commissions ! What do they know about our problems ? They always put people on them that don't know anything about coal, and people like that always end up by saying what the last person in their place said. That's why all these Commissions say the same thing. Let's get back to first principles." Stopping in the act of putting a portion of partridge in his mouth, he found something unexpectedly apt in his last phrase, and chewed that instead. " First principles— principles, mark you. Let's see what would happen if we amalgamated with the Paston Collieries next door. They've got two pits and a lot of obsolete equipment. First difficulty—valuation. They wouldn't accept ours, we wouldn't accept theirs, so the valuers would have to split the difference—and that'd mean over-capitalisation to start with. There's five directors on their board, and eight on ours. Our fees are higher than theirs. We wouldn't want to lose any of our directors, they wouldn't want to lose any of theirs. We'd probably end up with a board of twelve, at our level of fees. Their pits are high cost pits, and we'd have to shut down one of them at once. And that's amalgamation for you. We'd have to pay dividends on a lot of over-valued capital, we'd have four more hungry mouths to feed, and what we'd get out of it would be one pit. Whereas if we wait a few years more the concern will go bankrupt, and we'll be able to buy what we want at receiver's prices."

" Of course," Johnson said, " You're probably right— from your point of view. The real question is whether your point of view is the decisive one."

" What other point of view is there ? " Dinton demanded, his suave eyebrows raised.

" Well, there's the point of view that doesn't regard dividends and directors' fees as the final argument. The Coal Commission takes that view, I imagine. The miners do, certainly ! "

" The miners ! " burst out Mr. Starr. " The miners ! D'you know how much money I've got sunk in this company, young man ? Close on half a million ! But my view isn't decisive ! The miners' view is to be taken into account ! The wretched owner takes all the risks, he finds the money, bores, proves the seam, sinks a shaft and has all the trouble and anxiety. And then, when all that's done, in steps My Lord the Miner, with his own point of view ! "

" You don't think the miner, who after all risks his life even if he doesn't risk his money, is entitled to a point of view ? "

" He's entitled to the best safety precautions we can devise, and good pay if he works hard. That's what any man's entitled to. But he's not entitled to try to run my business for me, and if he tries to I'll fight him every inch of the way!"

Johnson shrugged. "The miner may not be entitled to his viewpoint, but he's got it. Whether you like it or not, it's become an important element in the coal trade. As for your fighting it, that's where the national viewpoint comes in. All this fighting has cost the country a lot of money. Thirty millions for a subsidy in '26, and an indirect loss of about three hundred millions through the stoppage. Then the unemployment that followed, with the slump, cost another three hundred millions in doles and charities. And now, in wartime, the Government is having to subsidise the industry again, to the tune of about a million a month. By and large this industry of yours has cost the country, in less than twenty years, about three times as much as its capital value. Whether you scrap with the miners, or the miners scrap with you, the country foots the bill. It's getting tired, because the bill gets bigger and bigger every year. In *The Times* the other day there was a letter from one of your coal owners saying that if the country wants a really efficient coal industry, the Government will have to advance two hundred millions to modernise it. The best economic opinion in the country seems to think that amalgamations between you smaller owners would make for efficiency. But if you reject that out of hand, you mustn't blame people if they start thinking that nationalisation is the only alternative!"

"Nationalisation, eh?" Mr. Starr leaned back, a thin smile on his lips, his heavy lids closed over his yellow eyes. "You think you could run this industry from Whitehall, eh?"

"Well, Mr. Starr, you run it from Cadogan Square."

"I can take risks and use enterprise in Cadogan Square. Have you ever known the Treasury be enterprising or take risks?"

" At this very moment, Mr. Starr, the Treasury is advancing money to the Coal Charges Account as loans at four per cent. interest. Before the account is closed, it'll probably be in the neighbourhood of forty or fifty million pounds. That's a risk no ordinary investor would take, as you know very well. Besides, most of the risks involved in mining are the creation of private enterprise. Under public ownership they would disappear. The export and home markets would be stabilised, for instance, and the risk of over-production eliminated. With that the risk of unemployment in the industry would largely disappear. Taking risks has no merit in itself, Mr. Starr, and when failure might affect the lives of a hundred thousand men, it's positively undesirable ! "

It had become clear by this time that the table talk had taken a thoroughly unsociable turn. Johnson, regretting his attacks, turned an appealing eye on his hostess, hoping she would take advantage of the outraged silence that followed his words to turn the conversation. But instead her eye met his with a covert, twinkling encouragement.

It was Dinton who broke the silence. He was younger than either of his fellow-directors, with a man-of-the-world air that suggested the politician. He broke into the talk with a light laugh.

" Of course I agree with a lot of what you say, Mr. Johnson. You mustn't take much notice of old Starr here—he's a notorious Diehard. Something's got to be done to ensure the miner a fair standard of living—that's agreed. But surely you don't really think you can do that by handing the mines over to the miners ? Because that's what your nationalisation would mean. Miners *versus* Bureaucrats, instead of Miners *versus* The Coalowners. Their demand for higher and higher wages would go on, and without private enterprise to cut down other production costs all the money would come out of the consumer's pockets. A Government may be able to avoid risks, but it's yet to be proved that it can be enterprising.   Or efficient in the business sense."

Johnson essayed a light laugh himself.   " The other day a miner told me that when he was a boy they used to call the pitheap at East Tanthope ' Charity Main,' because the miners used to be able to scrape a little free coal from it.   It struck me then that it would be a good name for the whole coalfield to-day.   It's years since any of you owners have risked putting any fresh capital or enterprise into these pits.   You've been scraping a little free dividends out of the capital your fathers invested.   Since the war you've all been guaranteed by the Government 1/6 a ton on the coals you raise.   Yet in spite of the preposterous price of coal, there's not a single pit in the county that's been able to earn that amount.   You've been subsidised by the Midlands coalfields.   The Midlands aren't prepared to go on doing that.   If it weren't that the money would otherwise go in Excess Profits Tax they wouldn't be prepared to do it now.   Pits like yours have been living for years on subsidies, plain or disguised.   It's been very enterprising of you to get so much out of so little.   It would be very enterprising of you now to hang on, fighting off nationalisation, in the hope of getting still more subsidies. But the country is beginning to see through such enterprise. It feels that your financiers have been enterprising too long—that it's now high time the technicians and research workers were given a chance to be enterprising."

Ten minutes later, as the front door closed behind him, Johnson could hear the old Major already making apologies for him.

Perhaps, he thought, he should have made the apologies himself.   Everything he had said over that lovely Sheraton table must have sounded abominably crude and harsh and graceless.   Every word a personal insult.   By now, no doubt, they were explaining him away as a ' theorist,' an ' intellectual,' even a ' damned Bolshie.'   Yet, with but the slightest change of emphasis, everything he had said might have been said by any member of the Tory Reform Committee. It seemed hardly credible that men whose interests were so bound up with coal could remain so completely oblivious of the forces that more and more dominated their situation. Yet was it surprising? The Starrs had been coalowners now for five generations. For more than a hundred years they had been able to take it for granted that their interests and those of the nation were inextricably one. Throughout their whole history as a coalowning family the one serious conflict of interests they had been faced with was the recurrent conflict with their workmen. To the present Mr. Starr, bred in a strong and positive family tradition, there was nothing in the present state of the industry that could not be interpreted in those terms. If the coal trade was in ruins, it was the fault of My Lord the Miner. If prosperity was to be restored to the trade, the country must help him to defeat My Lord the Miner. No other view of the situation could penetrate a mind dedicated from birth to a century-old family vendetta.

Chapter Eight

THE COMMITTEE

ONCE a week, in every colliery in the county, an interesting ceremony took place. A group of men, composed of four or five representatives of the workmen and an equal number of officials, would sit round a table in one of the colliery offices and go through certain ritual proceedings.

The proceedings would begin by one of the men, secretary of the group, passing slips of paper to the others, and as each man put his signature to the paper he would be handed three shillings. As soon as these transactions were completed one of the group would take a seat at the head of the table—not always the same man, for it was part of the ritual that each ' side ' of the group should have its representative in the Chair (as this particular seat is called) on alternate weeks.

At this point the rites varied. In many cases the man at the head of the table would now ask, " Does anyone wish to raise anything ? " Whereupon, receiving negative shakes of the head all round, he would stand up and say jocularly, " Well, that's that." When the group would leave the table and drift away talking.

In other cases the proceedings were less perfunctory. One of the group would begin to read out a series of figures from a ledger. Occasionally one of the workmen would interrupt him to make an observation.

" Ah'm told it's a bit clarty in th'Busty this week."

" That conveyor in the second North wants lookin' at— they's been several breakdowns lately."

It is at this point that the observer would notice certain subtle differences of attitude to the procedure as between the workmen and the officials. He would get the impression that the officials slightly resented the presence of the others, and wished to get through the ritual with as few interruptions as possible. Nevertheless if a comment was made by one of the workmen, one of the officials would within a minute or two also make occasion to speak.

" New Maudlin was late in getting away this week— three cutter men idle on Monday."

As it became clear that such remarks were intended to account for shortcomings in the week's output of coal, the observer would also notice another peculiarity of the group. Each side sought its explanations in different and quite unrelated terms. The workmen in the group called attention only to shortcomings in the equipment or layout of the pit. The officials called attention only to shortcomings in the workmen.

Occasionally some discussion would follow these remarks, in which specific remedies for the failures would be suggested. Almost invariably, if the suggestion came from an official, the workmen would subject it to hostile criticism, and if the suggestion came from the workmen, the officials would deal no less summarily with it. In the great majority of cases, after twenty minutes or half an hour of these interchanges, the reading of figures ceased, the man at the head of the table stood up, and the group dispersed.

It is notoriously difficult to discover the real social function of an institution merely from observation of the ceremonial associated with it. Johnson himself, after he had witnessed a few of these weekly gatherings, found it hard to persuade himself that what he saw was the working of that latest and greatest experiment in industrial democracy, the pit production committee. For years these committees had been demanded by the miners' leaders as essential for the improvement of relations between the two sides of the industry, as channels through which the stifled initiative and inventiveness of the workers could find expression, as means for affording each man in the pit a comprehensive view of his place and importance in the hierarchy of production. Yet here the committees were, and this was how they worked. Why did the achievement fall so short of its mark? Why, in fact, did the establishment of a pit production committee in so many cases only exacerbate, rather than improve, bad relations between men and management? It was to find an answer, and if possible to produce a remedy, that Johnson had been sent into the region.

There was an obvious temptation to say that the fault lay with the colliery managers. Indeed the case of the New Main pit production committee seemed to prove the point. It was the only committee in the county with a really constructive attitude to its work—a committee that had the characteristics of a research team. There was no doubt at all that the credit for the brilliant work of this committee was due to the vehement Steve Joyce, who with infinite patience and enthusiasm had informed and moulded the minds of the workmen's representatives, and of his own officials, until it really could undertake the functions it was intended for. He had kept the workmen fully informed about his plans—nay, more, he had explained why and how he had arrived at them. He had taught them to read working plans so that they could follow him, he had produced his little clay models for them to pore over with him. Often, if the workmen pressed for the adoption of a pet suggestion, he had put it into operation, against his own better judgment, so that they could not suspect him of ulterior motives ; and he waited until they themselves confessed its failure. He had taught them the cardinal points of scientific thinking : to define their problems clearly, to obtain all the relevant facts concerning them, and to try to arrive at solutions that did not go beyond either the terms or the facts of the problems. One at a time he had sent them, at the firm's expense, for six-week courses of training at the Sheffield Mechanisation Centre. He had encouraged them to suck his brain, and he had frankly picked theirs for all he was worth. Above all, he had treated them throughout, not as workmen, but as colleagues. Johnson spent many evenings listening to the discussions of the New Main production committee, marvelling at their frankness and clarity, waiting in vain for the slightest sign of partisan feeling. Yes, it was tempting to say that because an ardent colliery manager had here produced a good committee, managers were also responsible for the bad ones. Few managers indeed there were who regarded the committees as anything but a waste of their time. For the most part they said readily that they found absurd the idea that a workman could contribute anything of value to a discussion of production problems. They resented having to tell the men of their plans for future work, they resented as an infringement of their professional status the right of any Tom, Dick or Harry to criticise their doings. All that was to be expected. What was not to be expected was that the workmen, who had fought so long for these committees, should have proved so indifferent to their success when at last they were achieved. Had there been one workman's representative in the county who was trying, with the same ardour and patience as Steve Joyce, to make a success of his committee, then one could have set one's mind at rest. But there was not. There were many men who said they 'believed' in pit production committees, who expected great results from them if only the workmen were given more power on them. But never once did Johnson meet a man from the workers' side of the committees who was prepared, fully and unreservedly, to do his utmost within the existing constitution.

What were the powers of the workmen on the committee ? Since the function of the committee was to advise on matters of production, it had no direct powers. (Certain non-technical duties, like the allocation of extra clothing coupons and various permits had been given to the committees, to increase their standing with the body of workmen.) The committee could not take a vote on any matter falling under its notice. But the minutes of the meetings were forwarded weekly to the regional offices of the Ministry, where dissentient opinions about matters of any importance were earmarked for the attention of the production directors. By the constitution of the committee, the manager was required to give any information relevant to the matters discussed. The committee, or any single member of it, had the right to call the attention of the Regional Controller to any matter on which it was felt that action by the Ministry was desirable. The workmen, then, had every opportunity to take their grievances to a higher level—a level at which, it is true, the same basic dissensions prevailed and would probably stultify action, but where also there were half a dozen ex-trade union officials waiting to press for action.

But it was a rare thing for the workmen to make use of these constitutional rights. Indeed, they had a positive indifference to them. Nor were the reasons far to seek. Although the workmen's representatives on the production committees were supposed directly to represent the workmen, they were in fact chosen as representatives of the union. The distinction, in so highly organised an industry, may appear a fine one, but it was in fact very real. For the obvious representatives of the union were the Lodge officials. These men had been primarily chosen for their ability to negotiate in matters of dispute. Their habitual attitude to the management was either defensive or aggressive. They were on every pit deputation, every price and urgency committee. They were trained to present demands, to conceal facts that might embarrass their case, to hunt for facts to embarrass the other party. Inevitably they carried over into the pit production committees the struggles and suspicions that characterised the bulk of their work. In most of the larger pits at least two of the Lodge officials were employed practically full time on union affairs, and so seldom went underground. Familiar with the prices and compensable conditions of the working places, they were often quite unfamiliar with the technical position, and in discussion of production matters had usually to rely on second-hand information. Often, too, their duties kept them out of touch with large sections of the workmen : it was quite a normal thing at a pit production meeting to hear the Lodge Secretary ask the manager, " Have the men been complaining about anything this week ? " Such men were obviously unlikely to be fitted for detached and informed investigation of problems.

At a deeper level, too, their traditions prevented them from making full use of the production committees. They had inherited a complicated machinery of negotiation with the owners ; a machinery that took for granted a narrow, restricted range of interests. They had become experts in the use of this machinery, they knew just what they could get from it and how. The Ministry was something new to them, a third and unknown group of interests. They were even more suspicious of it than they were of the owners. When they had disputes with the owners, the only people they were used to notify, apart from the owners themselves, were their agents at the union headquarters. Their agents were not interested in production matters, but the feeling that it might perhaps be a rash and unwise thing to deal with a Ministry except through their agents persisted. The Ministry, to them, had become just another group to bargain with—a group with odd, not wholly assimilated habits and attitudes. It was, however, a source of money. The Ministry paid three shillings a week to pit production committee members. It could sometimes be persuaded to pay deputations for lost time. Thus some very odd situations came about. On one occasion, when a local Lodge was having a fierce dispute about transport allowances with the owners—a dispute which only the Ministry was empowered to decide—the Lodge officials refused to bring their case before the Regional Controller unless a shift's wages were paid to each member of the men's deputation ! But there was no money to be made out of writing a minority report to the Ministry on production matters. Therefore the reports were not written.

It is fair to add that the whole coalfield could not but be aware of the impotence of the Ministry, with its ' dual control,' on any issue of importance. Most Lodge officials suspected, and quite rightly, that even if issues were presented to the Controller, no action would be taken, because he would hand the matter over to his production department, which was staffed with coalowners' friends. What they did not realise was that the relative strength of the two parties in the Ministerial cockpit was determined, to some extent at least, by the support they received from outside. The production divisions could almost invariably rely on the active support of the coalowners. The labour divisions were left almost powerless by the failure of the miners to work with and through them.

Here, then, Johnson felt, was something he could do. Insofar as the failure of the pit production committees arose from their reluctance to report to the Ministry, and insofar as this reluctance derived from a lack of effective action by the Ministry, he could use his influence in the office to improve the situation.

His aim was to convince the committees that attention was paid to their deliberations, and that any issue brought to their notice would be taken up by the Ministry's officers with promptitude and impartiality. To begin with, he confined himself to issues that he could deal with himself. Whenever in the committee minutes he found reference to an unresolved conflict where he felt his intervention might be effective, he made a point of being present at the next meeting of the committee concerned. In this way he had one or two small but quite promising successes. He developed quite a competent technique, for example, in dealing with the problem of air pressure.

Air pressure was one of the most frequent sources of conflict. Every week, in scores of minutes, the men would complain that the air compressors were not working at full efficiency, and that therefore the cuttermen and hewers were being hampered in their work. Since in all but naked light pits the safest and therefore most general method of transmitting power to the coal face is by compressed air, the question was really an important one.

Almost invariably, when Johnson looked into these

complaints, he found that the facts themselves were being fiercely disputed, for neither the management nor the men had kept records to substantiate their statements. So it was always possible for Johnson, after explaining to the committee that he had come to investigate the workmen's complaints, to cause a mild sensation simply by saying :

" Now, can I have a look at the evidence ? "

The men would usually insist that the statements of the men at the coal face were evidence enough. The manager would usually say that the pressure was checked constantly on the main ranges, and that losses of pressure on subsidiary ranges were due to men carelessly or wilfully leaving valves open. But Johnson would stubbornly demand evidence of both contentions. He would illustrate the value of precise evidence by adducing some of his own.

" Seventeen times this year the question of air pressure has been raised in this committee. I went through the minutes yesterday and counted. Assuming that the ten of you have spent at least five minutes discussing the matter on each occasion, that means that about fifteen man-hours of your time has been spent on the problem, without getting any nearer a solution. If only a couple of hours had been devoted to collecting some reliable facts, think of the time and trouble you would have saved yourself."

Five minutes of lofty nagging in this fashion would usually drive both sides to self-justification. Then, unbending, Johnson would throw out suggestions to each side. The men should demand that the manager should get his maintenance men to make leakage tests of the compressed air system at regular intervals, and present their reports to the committee. The manager should insist that the men accompany all complaints with records of pressure-gauge readings. Usually, before he left, the committee would be getting down to questions about the best way to obtain the required data and at what intervals to present it.

A fortnight later, if nothing emerged in the meantime,

he would write to the committee asking for the results of its enquiries.

There was one obvious danger to this method of propagating the use of elementary research methods in the committees : that sooner or later it would bring to light a situation which the management could not or would not remedy, and where the Ministry's willingness to intervene would be put dangerously to the test. The situation was not slow in materialising. At one of the collieries the workmen's representatives, encouraged by Johnson, collected indisputable evidence of a grossly inefficient air compression system. The main compressor was old and worn beyond repair, the pipes leaked at every joint, there was bad overloading on some of the branch ranges. Johnson happened to be present at the committee meeting when the evidence was presented to the manager. The man hedged for a while, and then said that he had had a new air compressor and piping on order for some months, and was waiting delivery. Johnson remarked that if the committee sent a letter to the Mining Supplies Officer he could without doubt expedite the matter—whereupon the manager said, rather too quickly, that he had himself written recently.

The Supplies Division was a semi-autonomous section of the Ministry, with its own offices and staff ; and Johnson normally saw very little of its work and officers. But the following day, with a vague suspicion at the back of his mind, he rang up the regional Supplies Officer and asked if anything could be done about the air compressor on order for the X colliery. After ransacking his files, the Supplies Officer reported that he had no correspondence on that subject, and precious little on any other, from the colliery in question.

It was clear that the manager had invented the story of the ordered air compressor on the spur of the moment. What was to be done about it ? The question was really one for the production department ; Johnson had already exceeded his duties even by inquiring into the matter. He decided to wait for the arrival of the minutes recording the men's evidence and the manager's reply to it, and then pass the whole matter over to young Trunder.

A week later he learned that young Trunder had passed the matter on to the Group Production Director responsible, by word of mouth. After letting the matter rest for a fortnight, he inquired tactfully of the G.P.D. if any action had been taken on the matter, and received a markedly non-committal answer. Young Trunder told him that he had been reprimanded for taking the matter up at all, the official explanation being that the colliery manager had made an unintentional mistake. Trunder also gave him the unofficial and more likely explanation. The owners of X colliery were reluctant to replace old equipment with new while the future of the industry was so uncertain, and they had given the manager strict instructions to make the best of the existing equipment. Since the Ministry had no legal authority to order replacements, unless it was prepared to pay the cost, to pursue the matter further would only embarrass the manager without achieving anything more.

After this experience, Johnson put rather less enthusiasm into his advocacy of analytic methods of tackling production problems. Instead he turned his attention to those instances where new developments were already planned and opposition was likely to come rather from the workmen than the owners.

For the past year plans had been slowly maturing in the county for a number of mechanised-mining schemes, financed by Government loans. Three or four of these were on a really ambitious scale, making use of American lend-lease equipment; others were less spectacular, amounting to little more than a rationalisation of the haulage system in a particular seam, or power-loading on to a conveyor-belt. But all these schemes required radical changes in the working habits of the men employed on them, and some of them required a positive effort to learn new techniques and responsibilities, and the development of methods of group training.

The first of these new development schemes went into operation when Johnson had been in the coalfield only a month or two, and before he had really had time to appreciate what was happening. There was trouble from the very beginning. The company demanded that no new wage negotiations should be entered into for the new classes of work while the scheme was still in an experimental stage, and later, when provisional rates had at last been fixed, refused to commit itself as to the limit of the experimental period. The faults were not all on the one side. The men had stood out at first for piece-rate payments on the old tonnage basis, and even their own agents had had difficulty in persuading them to negotiate on the basis of a day-wage. When these preliminary difficulties had been overcome, the lack of any intelligent training of the new working groups soon made itself felt. The work at the face required the close co-operation of a team of six men. The absence of one would seriously embarrass the operations of an entire shift—unlike longwall mining, where one filler missing from twenty or more on the face made not too much difference. But the men working on the new scheme were slow to change their old habits. They still, on Mondays and Fridays, came to work only ' if they felt like it.' They carried over into the work their old luddite suspicion that advances in technique meant redundant workmen and speeded-up work. The management at the colliery had done little or nothing to induce any more positive attitude. The pit production committee had barely interested itself in the matter.

Here, then, was a job of work ripe for an Industrial Relations Officer. Johnson could devote himself to the task of laying the psychological and social groundwork for the success of these state-aided schemes. It was a clear field for the exercise of man-management techniques— the perfect experimental field, with clearly defined limits, so that one would be able to measure the success or failure of those techniques.

He had to wait a month or two for the next development scheme in the county; but he prepared himself zealously for the event. It was to be introduced at a colliery called Fillingworth, in the southern part of the coalfield—a modest scheme, working short stalls of coal in a thin seam with Arcwall cutters and a drastically rationalised haulage system to reduce the proportion of unproductive labour. The production department was keen on the development, which promised new possibilities in seams of coal too thin for standard power-loading practice. Young Trunder was advising on the special plant required, and made frequent journeys out to consult with the manager. Johnson joined him as often as his other work would permit.

The colliery lay at the edge of a great area of flooded coal—flooding brought about by ruthless working of seams in the westerly hills in a way that allowed the water to drain away to the collieries at lower levels. Two or three collieries had already been abandoned in this area; the Fillingworth pit had already had one seam flooded, and was only keeping open the rest of its workings by incessant pumping. It was a country of lovely wooded foothills and broad streams, pockmarked with the most stricken villages in the whole county. With the coming of the railways several large collieries had been opened in the district to work the excellent coking coals lying beneath the surface; but in the past twenty or thirty years the flood menace had grown to such proportions that, even in those collieries remaining in a workable condition, added costs of piecemeal pumping were such that they could only operate in periods of heavy demand. The little village of Fillingworth, lying in a fold of land two miles from the main road, was a huddle of miners' rows with unmade streets, patches of waste ground littered with brickbats where cottages had rotted on their own foundations without anyone having reason to clear them away, a co-op. stores and a pawnshop. For six years in the depression the colliery had been closed. Between 1937, when it reopened, and the outbreak of war, there had never been less than 40 per cent. registered unemployment. The little community of four thousand people, with regular work now for the first time in a generation, scarcely knew what to do with its prosperity.

The manager of the colliery was young, and intensely ambitious. In pre-war days he would have been building up a reputation for ruthless cost-cutting at the expense of his labour; to-day he saw that reputations would be built on the capacity for long term planning. When Johnson first met him, he was deploring the fact that his first serious effort in this direction should have to take place in a colliery where the chances of success were so small.

" Why ? " Johnson asked.

" Fillingworth miners have got long memories," the manager said glumly. " They remember that when conveyors first came to the pit thirty years ago, sixty putters were immediately sacked. When pneumatic picks came, the hewers wages went down. They don't like progress in this village. They only see the ogre at the heart of it."

Johnson studied the pit, went underground with the manager on his tours of inspection, spent a few evenings with the men in their club, talked with the Lodge officials. More particularly, he familiarised himself with every detail of the new development scheme. When these details were finally settled, and the day came for the pit production committee to be informed about it, he was present at the meeting.

The men's representatives received the manager's outline

without any change of expression : they were a grim set of men anyhow.

" Tha means tha'll sack half the datal hands in the Ballarat," the Lodge Secretary said bluntly. ' Datal ' workers are those on day-wages, principally haulage hands.

" Not sack them. Upgrade them to productive work," the manager said.

" Aye," the Lodge Secretary said, ambiguously brief. " We'll tell the Lodge."

Johnson butted in. " I've spent a fortnight swotting up the details of this scheme—and it's not my future that's at stake on it. You've sat here for ten minutes listening to Mr. Harris, and haven't asked a single question about it. Why not find out something about the scheme before you tell the Lodge."

" If they's owt else ta knaw, tha can tell us," the Lodge Secretary conceded.

In the technical talk that followed, the hostility of the men abated a little, or rather sought to express itself in criticism of the details of the scheme. Mr. Harris, the manager, was wily enough to concede one or two small points to them ; and there were other points they raised the relevance of which was uncertain from the information available on the plans. Johnson, borrowing a leaf from Steve Joyce's book, suggested that a clay contour model of the experimental district should be made to scale, and discussed more fully at the next meeting. The idea was taken up at once. Johnson also offered to bring along to the next meeting a film projector and some technical films illustrating some of the problems of haulage layout. That too was accepted.

So it came about that within a month, and by the time the first of the new equipment began to arrive at the pit, the men's representatives were more than half convinced that the new development scheme was more than an attempt to cut labour costs. No less important, Mr. Harris was

beginning to see the point of taking pains to secure the
active interest of the men.   The next step was to precipitate
all this half-formed goodwill into a definite co-operative
venture.

Johnson was anxious that news of the development
should not reach the body of workmen only through the
medium of the Lodge.   His idea was that the pit production
committee should, as a corporate body, call a meeting of the
men, explain the whole scheme to them as endorsed by the
whole committee, meet frankly all criticisms and suspicions,
and demand full and active interest.   Especially he wanted
it explained to them that the interests of the nation were so
deeply involved in the success of the scheme that the
Government itself was meeting most of the costs.

That was where the main difficulty came.   The details
of these ' capital assistance ' transactions between Ministry
and coalowners were being kept secret—at the wish of the
coalowners.   Johnson knew that he would readily get
permission to divulge so open a state secret if the company
itself raised no objection.   But Mr. Harris shook his head
dubiously when Johnson suggested this.

" My directors wouldn't like that a bit," he said unhappily.
" I can see your point, of course.   The men might put their
backs into it more if they know they're not just working for
profit.   But the directors don't like the men to have any
knowledge of the financial transactions of the company.
I don't think they'd see any reason for it.   And I couldn't
take the responsibility on myself."

The managing director of the company lived in the
county town :   Johnson telephoned him.   The voice
uttered an exclamation of polite incredulity as he explained
his requirements.   " I'm afraid that wouldn't be policy,"
it repeated to every argument ;   and as Johnson pressed
further added, " Besides, I'd have to consult the Board,
and it won't be meeting for a month."

So the meeting was held without permission being

obtained to exchange the final confidences. It was held in the upstairs hall of the miners' club. Johnson had prepared large diagrams of the scheme, so that the audience could follow the speeches easily; the clay model was set out on a table near the door; and there was a projector with slides to illustrate details. As Mr. Harris said, as he nervously watched the miners coming into the hall and staring inscrutably about them, " This is the first time in the history of the whole coalfield that so much trouble's been taken to get the co-operation of the men. I hope they don't think we're trying to trick them into something ! "

Johnson had been invited to take the Chair; he sat in the centre of a semi-lune, with the four representatives of the management on one hand and the four representatives of the workmen on the other. Before him, packed tight on wooden forms, three or four hundred pale expressionless faces watched him. At five minutes past the hour he tapped on the card table which was his emblem of office, and stood.

It was the first time he had addressed an audience of miners on so formal an occasion, and he began nervously. He spoke about the woebegone state of the coal industry, and the responsibility that his Ministry had inherited. He got a few laughs when he said, " Nobody likes my Ministry. The coalowners don't like it because they can't have their own way with it. The miners don't like it because *they* can't have their own way with it. We're called meddlesome bureaucrats if we try to impose controls, and maundering bureaucrats if we don't. Well, at least we control our tempers. . . ."

He went on to paint a picture of the fortunes of Filling-worth colliery since the last war, with its constant struggle against flood-waters, its grinding poverty and unemployment. Then he talked about the future of the pit.

" About the immediate future," he said, " there's less uncertainty for you than for most people. The Government have guaranteed your wage rates and employment for another four years. I'm not going to say it's taking much of a risk in doing so. Because it's certain that for the next four years Europe will need all the coal it can get. But what about the fifth year, and the years following it ? "

Mr. Harris was going to tell them about a development scheme that he and the production committee had been working on. The scheme had the full approval of his Ministry, and it was being watched with great interest as the forerunner of many such schemes. If the scheme was successful, it might considerably lower the working costs and increase the output of Fillingworth pit. But to be successful it needed the full co-operation of everyone working in the pit—not just passive consent, but active interest, help and suggestions for improvement. That was the purpose of to-night's meeting : to discuss the matter in the light of every man's practical experience.

" There's no eyewash about this," he finished up. " The results of this meeting can make or break the fortunes of this pit and everyone present. So if you've any doubts about Mr. Harris's scheme, when he's explained it to you, then stand right up and say so. And if you haven't any doubts, then stand up also and tell him you're backing him with all your energy and brains. But be frank and honest ; don't go away with reservations, even if you have to stay all night. Because it's important. The way you act to-night may decide whether or not your kids have enough to eat in six or seven years' time ! "

Johnson was clapped quite heartily when he sat down to make way for the manager, and he knew that he had been personally successful. But to appeal for frankness and honesty, when he could not be completely frank and honest himself, left a bitter taste in his mouth. He listened glumly while Mr. Harris spoke, pinning up a diagram to a blackboard and tracing the whole development through from the coal face to the pithead. When he had finished, Johnson introduced the Lodge Secretary, who said that thinking about this scheme had kept him awake at nights, but he was convinced that it was vitally necessary, and he had co-operated to the utmost on the pit production committee. Now he implored the men to rally behind the committee and make a real success of it.

When he, too, sat down, Johnson stood up again. "We'll take questions one at a time, and Mr. Harris will answer them."

There was silence. His eyes moved slowly over the rows of white faces, lined, thoughtful faces, and as he watched he saw the expressions, uncertain at first, harden upon them: sullenness, suspicion, hostility. Johnson turned to the Lodge Secretary beside him, who shrugged slightly, then stood up.

"Eh, tha, Dick Reay," he said, looking straight at an old man in one of the front rows, "Tha's got plenty ta say fer thasel' maist times—let's ha'e a bit crack from tha noo!"

The old man hesitated, then rose from his seat with rheumaticky movements. "Mister Chairman," he said slowly, "Ah divvent knaw what ma marrows feel. But me, Ah feel we ought ta discuss this business in oor Lodge first." There was a full-throated chorus of agreement as he sat down.

That was what Johnson had gone to all this trouble to avoid—the technical future of the pit being decided in the narrow, prejudice-heated atmosphere of a Lodge meeting. Baffled and defeated, he sank into his chair— and then, scarcely knowing what he was doing, he sprang up again.

"There's a very good reason why I should ask you to discuss it here, and not in your Lodge meeting. This isn't just a matter between you and the owners. My Ministry's got a voice in it too. The greater part of the cost of this scheme is being paid out of public funds. The country is putting in forty thousand pounds, in the hope that it will be for the benefit of the entire industry, not

just for the owners. That's why I'm here to-night, and
that's why I implore you not to let the country down ! "

He sat down amid a buzz of talk, carefully avoiding the
manager's eye. The Lodge Secretary leaned over to him
and said, " If tha'd told me that before tha'd ha'e saved a
lot of trouble ! " At the back of the hall three men rose to
their feet. " Mister Chairman," they said simultaneously.

The meeting closed an hour and a half later with a
resolution for the utmost support of the men in the new
scheme.

Chapter Nine

THE SACK

IT was considered, in the Regional offices, as the last
straw that a local reporter should have been present at
the Fillingworth meeting. At the week-end the *County
Chronicle* carried the full story under a streamer headline :
Government Aid for Local Pit. The owners, incensed
beyond measure, laid their complaints both regionally and
nationally, through their organisation. The Financial
Section of London headquarters sent an incredulous letter
to the Regional Controller, asking for an explanation of
this unprecedented breach of confidence. Johnson was
stared at, questioned in sepulchral tones. Then, after an
embarrassed silence of two days, he was asked to prepare
a report on his work in the Region during the nine months
of his office. It was quite obvious that this was regarded
as an opportunity for him to tender his resignation.

So for four hours Johnson sat at his desk dictating, to a
buxom little girl who stared at him with round excited eyes
whenever he paused to seek a word, his considered views
on the industry. It was an odd experience this, the last
significant official act he would make. His report would

be read, he knew, for one phrase only—the last. But because a certain scandal now attached to him, it would be read. He was determined to write a report that would remain in their memories.

The finished document read thus :

REPORT OF INDUSTRIAL RELATIONS OFFICER

1. It will be recalled that at the time of my appointment, in April of this year, the widespread strikes resulting from the Porter Awards were in process of settlement. The terms of settlement, as embodied in the National Wage Agreement, were generous to the miners : but it was obvious to everyone that, while the Agreement would probably succeed in reducing the number of disputes to the minimum during the four years of its bond, it was unlikely in itself to affect the underlying causes of dispute. Indeed, the coalowners widely predicted that the Agreement would have the direct effect of encouraging absenteeism and restriction, and so reduce output still further. My appointment in an experimental capacity at this time encouraged me to believe that my real duties were to take advantage of the four-year armistice, first to assess the industrial, social and psychological causes responsible for the notoriously bad relations between miners and coal-owners, and secondly to experiment with techniques for removing the causes or mitigating their effects.

2. I was chosen for this work on my record as a trained sociologist with experience both in industrial research and practical labour organisation. My duties, as laid down by Headquarters, were deliberately framed to leave me with the utmost freedom, although I was specifically charged with improving the working of pit production committees and all industrial publicity in the region. Immediately upon taking up my duties, therefore, I reduced my office-work to a bare minimum and devoted my time to as close and intimate a study of the coalfield as was possible. In

the first three months of this investigation I visited thirty-four collieries in the county, some of them several times, discussed local conditions, grievances and customs with managers, trade union officials and workmen. During the course of these visits I spent rather more than seventy hours in underground visits at twelve different collieries, on three occasions working full shifts with the men at the coal face and on the haulage ways. I should like here to thank my colleagues in this office, whose advice and assistance on these visits were invaluable, for the trouble they put themselves to on my behalf. My findings have been given in many separate reports and memoranda, but I will give them again here in a correlated form.

3. This county now produces rather less than one-seventh of the national coal output with rather more than one-seventh of the total number of workers in the industry. Of nearly two hundred pits now working, more than ninety are more than a century old, while several shafts still in use were first sunk more than two hundred years ago. History is the *femme fatale* of the coal trade in more respects than one, and it is necessary to insist from the beginning on the great age, both of the workings and of the traditions, in these parts.

4. There are a hundred and ten villages and towns with a predominantly mining population scattered fairly equally over the five hundred square miles of this county. Although many of these villages are set in the heart of some of the loveliest country, they present an extraordinarily uniform picture of bleak ugliness to the stranger with standards set by South of England villages. There is another noteworthy peculiarity in the physical appearance of these villages. Wherever, by chance, the eye rests upon some building more attractive than its neighbours, one almost invariably finds that it owes its existence to the organised efforts of the miners themselves. Their clubs, welfare institutes, co-op. stores are the outstanding

institutional buildings. The charming little rows of cottages built for aged miners are also their handiwork ; and the occasional less charming but still outstanding housing estates built by local councils in the last twenty years owe their existence to the urgent representations of miners' representatives on these bodies. Conversely, wherever the eye selects some row of cottages as being more squalid and offensive than others, one invariably finds that these are colliery-owned cottages. There can be no question at all that these villages (most of which assumed their present size during the middle years of the nineteenth century) owe all their horror to the colliery-owners who built them, and all their redeeming features to the organisational energies of the people who live in them.

5. Of the collieries themselves I should perhaps say little, since I am no mining engineer. Yet my knowledge of general engineering processes leaves me in no doubt that all but half a dozen of the largest and newest pits in the county are worked to no very exacting technical standards. There is not a single colliery whose surface layout makes any pretensions either to efficiency or seemliness. The managers and their office staff conduct their complicated affairs in offices and with equipment that have remained unchanged since the last century. Nearly every manager with whom I have spoken has admitted that the underground layout of his pit, after twenty years of snatch working and ' quality grading,' has become an unmanageable honeycomb of ill-kept roads such as to make efficient underground transport impossible. Ventilation is bad, lighting is worse, and research to improve these and other technical deficiencies almost non-existent.

6. It is inevitable that any technical criticism of the pits should seem to reflect on the capacities of the managers. And it is true that the typical colliery manager in this county is not a very inspiring person. For two generations the industry has become less and less attractive to talented and

enterprising young men ; the prospect of living in a mining village, with such mines as these to control, has scared away from the industry all but those whose imaginations are too bounded to conceive anything better. Even so, the industry fails to make anything like the best use of the brains left over. The statutory qualifications required of a colliery manager are a sound grounding in mining technology ; but the odd development of the industry in recent years leaves him with less and less time to practise his competency in this field. Recently I persuaded two managers, both of medium-sized collieries employing about a thousand people, to make time-studies of their week's work for me. In the first case, 72 per cent. of the manager's working-hours (calculated at sixty hours) was spent dealing with labour problems of one sort or another—attendance at production committees, welfare committees, canteen committees, pit committees, absentee tribunals, National Service Officer appeal courts, deputations and sundry complaints ; leaving him only a few hours a week for his proper work of technical supervision and planning. In the second case, the manager contrived to delegate some of his committee-duties and so reduce his dealing with labour problems to a mere 60 per cent. of his time. While most of this work is necessary, it is absurd that it should be done by a man chosen for his qualifications in other fields. There is an obvious case for personnel managers at all collieries employing more than five hundred workmen : as it is there is not a single personnel manager in the county, even in the case of collieries employing three thousand or more men.

7. But it is not the colliery managers who administer this industry : it is the coalowners. They are an elusive breed, and therefore hard to study in their natural habitat. The four or five most powerful individual owners still living in the county have diverse interests and *grand seigneur* standards ; a minor civil servant does not meet them, and

must judge them by their visible works. But lest my worm's eye view of them should seem distorted, let me preface my own remarks by quoting a bishop who stayed in their houses, ate at their tables, shared their counsels and approved their politics. His summing-up runs thus :

" Mineowners, unlike most other great employers of labour, are not normally confronted by a local opinion and tradition which may stimulate the sense of social obligation, and restrain the shortsighted selfishness of acquisition. The minefield seemed to me significantly destitute of those evidences of serious effort by Capital to improve the conditions of Labour which so often arrest the attention in great cities. Often I heard the question, *Who ever met a poor mineowner?* There may be, probably there is, as much ignorance as reason in the challenge, and not all mineowners are alike ; but it cannot be disputed that *the wills of deceased coal magnates, even in bad times, go far to provide a certain justification for the popular belief.*"[1]

It is noteworthy that the good bishop assumes absentee ownership as a standard condition of the industry. In this he does something less than strict justice to that handful of local men who administer their interpenetrating interests in coal, steel, shipping, insurance and breweries from this city. But in checking up the place of residence of the twelve largest coalowners in this county I find that only three live inside the county, while no less than seven live in and about the industrial areas of Yorkshire. Of these twelve owners, eight at least are members of families associated with this coalfield for more than a hundred years ; and the implication of the admittedly inadequate figures given above would seem to be that profits earned in this coalfield have been gradually reinvested in the newer coalfields and industries to the south.

8. There can be no question that the coalowners of this county have manifested little sense of social responsibility

[1] *Retrospect of an Unimportant Life.*—H. H. Henson. Vol. 2, p. 406.

for the hundred thousand miners from whom their wealth derives. Nor have they shewn to any appreciable extent that spirit of enterprise and independence which they themselves advance as the chief justification for their existence. Singularly little fresh capital has been brought into the coalfield in the last two decades (apart from Government grants during the course of this war). What technical advances have been made in the same period have been concentrated entirely on the marketing rather than the production of coal. Sheltered under the price-fixing machinery of the 1930 Coal Act, and using unemployment benefits to keep an abundance of surplus labour always on hand, all their energies have been bent on price-cutting, i.e., wage reductions.

9. The long, strong traditions of ownership in these parts, indeed, almost inhibit any other response to economic problems than the attack on wages. The owners have inherited a proud and arrogant conception of their function from their great-grandfathers who made the Industrial Revolution. They remember that the railways of the world were the children of their brain, that the iron foundries of England grew up under their guidance and advice. Our modern industrial civilisation came to school in this part of the world, and in return made oligarchs of the industrialists it found here. Particularly, among the owners of to-day, the economic dogmas of the nineteenth century have survived almost untouched. Coal still ' tends towards a natural price,' and wages must still be pared ' in accordance with the law of supply and demand.' A long tradition of negotiating wage claims on the basis of the price of coal has made them almost incapable of the intellectual effort required to conceive of methods of reducing costs other than reducing wages. I have before me now a letter from one of the more influential owners, commenting on the reduced output of his collieries. " I am quite sure," he says, " there is no prospect of any increase

in the output so long as these high wages obtain. It must not be assumed that I am of the opinion that the men are not entitled to these high wages, as they are not unduly out of proportion to the wages got in other industries, but nevertheless the fact remains that the men generally find they have more than enough to meet their needs and want more leisure or an easier time. When the war is over, if these high wages remain and the present restrictions are removed, absenteeism will increase and there will be a further fall in output." It is quite clear that the author of this letter has never stopped to ask himself how other industries contrive to pay reasonable wages without suffering a decline of output, or wondered if the response of the miners might not be different if he relied less on manpower and more on horsepower.

10. The survival of these outmoded attitudes has been helped by the fact that most of the directors of colliery companies are technically unqualified, and are therefore dependent on their managers and agents for advice as to the practicability and profitability of applying new technical methods in their pits. It is natural for any man who depends on others for advice to feel less confident in the outcome than those who gave the advice. It is also natural for any man to give more weight to factors he understands than to those he doesn't, when summing up a situation. Hence the fact that, while the financial and market structure of the industry has been considerably integrated in the past twenty years, the technical picture has remained almost unchanged.

11. It is not surprising that, in the course of a century and a half during which the coal industry has been of central importance to the development of the country, the coalowners have come to identify the national interest with their own. During the first century of their dominance they asked no more than to be left alone—even though this allowed them to maim children, work men fourteen hours a day in poison

ous air, evade inspection of their workings, evict unionists from their homes and avoid paying compensation for injuries and death. But that was during a period of steadily expanding markets. With the contraction of their markets after the last war, their belief in the identity of national and coal-owning interests assumed a more positive form. They shewed an increasing tendency to rely upon the State to help them out of their difficulties. A twenty-odd million pound grant in 1925. Price-fixing legislation in 1930. Indirect subsidies of unemployment benefits which enabled them to close their pits for six months at a time and still have a labour-force when they were reopened. And now, since 1942, the generous arrangements of the Coal Charges Account, which empowers them to borrow from the Treasury at 4 per cent. in order to pay themselves a standard profit of 10 or 12 per cent. Meanwhile, using the 'future uncertainty of ownership' as their excuse, they are ceasing even to replace the necessary equipment of the pits, blaming the consequent reduction of output on the men, and telling the Government through their Associations that huge Government grants will be necessary after the war to bring the industry to a level of competitive efficiency. This, they say, will be necessary in the national interest. Of this there can be no doubt. Nor can there be any doubt that the present coalowners, of this county at least, are constitutionally and technically incapable of handling public monies for any purpose other than their own profit.

12. In turning to deal with the miners, I want first to call attention to the inherent peculiarities of their work. While only a small percentage of the men employed in the mines are actually engaged in coal-getting, it is the work at and around the coal face that determines the attitude of the whole mining community to mining as an occupation. The hewers, fillers, cutters and putters who work at or near the coal face, and are paid piece-rates for their output, are the most influential sections of the local Lodges, and a great

majority of the disputes arising in the pits are on questions solely affecting these sections. Piece-rates, in any industry, are always a fertile source of dispute, and this no doubt contributes to the peculiar unrest and bitterness characterising the relations inside the industry. But more important, I am convinced, is a psychological element inseparable from the occupational problems of mining. Operations in the dark and dust and heat of an underground tunnel subjected to tremendous geological pressures afford only a precarious margin of control over working conditions. The skilled factory worker is reasonably certain that, with the use of the appropriate technique, and the expenditure of a given amount of energy, he can produce the results required of him. But the skilled miner works in an incessantly shifting world of variables and incalculables. Seams dip and roll, get thinner or thicker, harder or softer. Roofs cave in without warning, floors heave, roads creep. Gob-fires, floods, gusts of poisonous gas are liable to interrupt work at any moment. The high accident rate of the industry is only the most tragic index to the unpredictable behaviour of nature underground : for every accident that harms a worker, there are a dozen that interfere with his work. No miner, however skilled and energetic, has any assurance that a given expenditure of skill and effort will produce a given quantity of coal.

13. This element of uncontrol in his work is, I am convinced, of central importance to the understanding of the mineworker's psychology. When conditions are favourable, his work is immensely satisfying. He has, what so few workers have to-day, a direct and immediate sense of the purpose of his every action. But just because the winning of coal can be so psychologically satisfying, the incessant interruptions and hindrances are that much more frustrating. No financial compensation, in the form of payments for exceptionally difficult work, can affect this basic frustration. That the paysheet sums the total of a

miner's interest in his work is an error which miners fall
into scarcely less often than coalowners : but it is an error
nevertheless. No one who has spent a few evenings
talking with miners in their clubs can help noticing the
peculiarly obsessive hold their work has on them. " They's
more cowels won in t'Club than iver they is in t'Pit," is a
comment most miners make at one time or another. It
can, I think, be accepted without question that the day-to-
day frustrations of mining account for much of this
obsessiveness.

14. It can also, I think, be held to account for something
more important. Few laws of human behaviour are more
firmly established than that which traces a causal connection
between frustration and aggression. Effort that fails to
achieve its object in one field of activity seeks, with increased
urgency, success in another field. " If I can't get my own
way here, I'll get it there." We take the reaction so much
for granted that half the stock situations of comedy are
based on it : the child, denied a second helping of pudding,
kicks the table ; the henpecked business man bullies his
typist ; the infirm poet writes swashbuckling verses. In
general, if we find people behaving in a peculiarly aggressive
fashion, we look for frustration in some other field of their
experience. (It is not often that the aggressor himself
provides the clue, as when Karl Marx, having finished the
first volume of *Das Kapital*, remarked with savage satisfaction : " That'll give the bourgeoisie cause to remember
my carbuncles ! ")

15. The stubborn, aggressive character of the miners
in their relations with the mineowners has been the subject
of constant comment. Disraeli, writing *Sybil* in the 1850's,
noticed it :

" Whenever the mining population is disturbed the
disorder is obstinate. On the whole they endure less
physical suffering than most of the working classes,
their wages being considerable ; and they are so brutalised

that they are more difficult to operate on than our reading and thinking population of the factories. But when they do stir there is always violence and a determined cause."
The Tory Reform Committee uses different language to-day, but the general tenor of their remarks is the same :

" Mining labour in general has a sour and suspicious outlook. The evidence, if any is needed, is that coal, with one-twentieth of the workpeople in industry, was responsible for two-thirds of the time lost in industrial disputes between the wars."

Without prejudice to the rights or wrongs of the miners' struggles it must be conceded that they prosecute their fight with a fervour and tenacity far beyond that of other sections of the organised workers with grievances no less cogent. Some explanation of this aggressive character is necessary to a full understanding of the industry, and it is my firm belief that the basic (though not the only) cause is to be found in the occupational frustrations inseparable from work in the mines.

16. This hypothesis—that the obduracy of the miner is a function of highly variable and uncontrollable working conditions—makes no attempt to account for the particular forms in which aggression dresses itself. For this, examination of the social circumstances of the mining community is necessary. Three factors are of decisive importance here. The social isolation of most mining villages : the industrial isolation, which makes the income of a whole village population dependent on the fortunes of a single pit ; and the physical isolation imposed by geography. The combination of these three factors has led the miners' unions to assume direct responsibility for many matters normally considered beyond the scope of trade unionism. The Union Lodge, in the ordinary mining village, is not just one of a number of social institutions of more or less importance ; it is *the* paramount institution, subsuming all others. If a man is elected to a Lodge office, he will also be elected

pretty certainly to the local parish council, the Welfare Institute committee, the management committee of the co-op. stores, the Workmen's Club committee, the Aged Miners' Homes committee, and as many other bodies as his constitution will stand. If a vicar wants to hold a garden fête, the local Labour Party to nominate a candidate, the Sports Club to arrange a fixture, the colliery band to accept an engagement, he will be consulted. To think of the miners' unions, therefore, simply as *trade* unions, in the way that one thinks of, say, the transport unions or the A.E.U., is fundamentally to misunderstand their nature. Their functions are much more like those of the local medieval church than any other modern institution.

17. This development has been made possible by the coalowners' complete severance of industrial from social responsibilities. Up to the late nineteenth century, whenever a new pit was opened, the owner built a few rows of houses around it to house the workers he required, and so called a village into being without any further thought of obligation. Some of these villages quickly became the size of small towns ; but from the point of view of social resources they remained worse equipped than rural hamlets. The uniformity of colliery housing and the lack of alternative sources of employment imposed a uniformity of living standards and styles which, crystallising into traditions, has been able to resist influences to which the rest of the country has long succumbed. Nowhere is this more noticeable, or of more immediate importance, than in the consumer-habits of the miners. In spite of all the efforts of modern advertising, the miners' needs remain essentially those of the last century. There is less 'conspicuous consumption,' less competitive parade of acquisitions, in a mining village than in any other community in the country. Even house furnishings are practically identical from one house to another. Thus a sharp increase in wages, as happened last year, does not produce the phenomenon,

so repellent to middle class wives, of working women wearing fur coats. The only commodity in which there is any wide elasticity of demand is beer. Because of this, the owners are undoubtedly right when they claim that increases in wages have an immediately depressing effect on production. The miner will not work at his uncongenial tasks beyond the need of his simple family requirements ; or if, from motives of patriotism, he does, his village offers him only one avenue of spending his unwonted earnings— the Club and the pub, where he is apt to drink himself so sick that he is too ill to come to work the following day.

18. The mining community, then, makes its demands on life *as* a community, and not as a collection of individuals. It adjusts itself to new situations in the same way. A lot can be learned about miners by studying their wallpaper. The first miner's home I ever stayed in had a pale wallpaper with a very subdued pattern in the parlour, and over this the housewife (all wallpapering in this part of the world is done by the wives as a normal part of their spring-cleaning) had pasted strips of a dark paper, to give the effect of panelling. In my innocence I took this to be an individual exercise in decor, and congratulated her. It was only later I found that practically every other cottage in the village had its parlour papered to produce exactly the same panelled effect. One day the co-op. store had produced a stock of dark stripped paper ; the housewives of the village had discussed it, approved it, and bought it ; the manager of that store now knew to a yard how much dark stripped paper he would sell every year. In the same way, innovations in mining practice are scrutinised by the miners as a body. If they approve, it is all well and good. If they disapprove, they will resist as long as they have power to do so. Past experience seems to suggest that the sort of innovation most likely to be resisted is (*a*) those that reduce the prestige and importance of face workers in relation to other classes of workers, and (*b*) those

that require some marked modification of traditional working customs, such as the cavil and bargain.

19. In the long-drawn intensity of their struggle for better conditions many of the familiar mechanisms of war psychology have become ingrained in the miner's habits of thought. The Owner as Enemy, for instance, has often become a symbol quite divorced from any relation to objective fact. I have frequently found in conversation with them that men who fiercely denounce the Owners, accusing them of the most ruthless and heartless malpractices, do not even know the names of the managing directors of the companies they work for. For the men they meet daily—the colliery managers and agents—they have usually the highest respect. It is the invisible ones, the shadowy figures dictating policies from distant cities, on whom they project the catalogue of enormities culled from a long history of battles. Convinced that the owners allow no scruples to stand in their way, the miners too have developed habits of unscrupulousness. They have a facile habit, for instance, of concealing demands made for purely financial reasons behind elaborate rationalisations about safety. The century-long tradition of strife, too, has made them less concerned about the immediate objectives of the struggle: I have been told—by the men concerned—of strikes that were embarked on because a coin came down heads instead of tails. And there is a story that, in the middle of the long-drawn stoppage of 1926, a local official approached the manager of the pit with a request that the owners should loan the Lodge a thousand pounds, because its strike funds had run out.

20. In this attempt to unravel some of the complicated springs of action peculiar to the miners, much is necessarily hypothesis and speculation. Although labour problems have long been advanced as the chief cause of declining production in the coal industry, there has been singularly little effort made to investigate the causes of mining unrest.

The miners have produced one set of explanations, the owners another; and the general public, and even the disinterested worker inside the Ministry, has had simply to choose between one or other of the interested parties. The Government has paid its wergild, sometimes to the miners, sometimes to the owners, to buy a year or two of peace. It has set up Commission after Commission to decide between the claims of one side and another, but has not, to my knowledge, spent a farthing on social research into this most disputed of hinterlands. To date the Government has paid, since the beginning of the war, some thirty million pounds to the owners to maintain their standard rate of profit; it has authorised heavy increases in the price of coal to pay higher wages; it is advancing more than eight millions to selected collieries for technical improvements and developments—and still production goes down, and still absenteeism is blamed. A team of research workers, bringing scientific training and an experimental approach to bear on the subject, might, at the cost of a few thousand pounds, save the country fruitless millions of further expense. Why have they never been set to work? Alas, one knows only too well. Nothing is done in this Ministry without the consent of both owners and miners. And both want to win their private war in their own way.

21. This Report will be seen by both the owners' representatives in this Ministry, and by the miners' representatives. That it will annoy the owners causes me little grief: they have prospered exceedingly from their exploitation of the nation's coal resources, and if they go they will leave little good behind them. But that I should find myself acting the candid friend to men with whom my sympathies are wholly engaged, who have achieved nothing from their centuries of labour but a wilderness of half-derelict homes overshadowed by pitheaps—this is not to my liking. Yet I know that both sides are now preparing for their final battle which, if either succeeds in imposing

its own terms on the other, will spell ruin for the country. The battle will be joined on the issue of the technical rehabilitation of the industry. The prize will be a hundred million or more of public funds: the cost to the Government of bringing the mines up to the technical level of their continental competitors. To spend this money on the pits, and allow the present system of ownership to continue, would be infamous. The owners have proved themselves wholly incapable, as a body, of departing from their traditional practices and obsessions. But any form of nationalisation which allowed the miners themselves executive responsibility for the running of the pits would be fatal: nothing is clearer than that their very history has unfitted them for this responsibility; they are far too prone to pull off the tablecloth to get at the cake. Any form of nationalisation that does not meet their vague demands of ' The Mines for the Miners,' however, will have to face opposition from the miners—an opposition shaped and sharpened in the hells they have lived through. Sympathy and understanding will be necessary, firmness and preparation too. Now rather than later is the time to prepare. In the next year or so the Ministry will be initiating, at one colliery after another, a series of mechanisation and development schemes—forerunners of the great reorganisation to come. They are the fruits of public finance and public enterprise. They should be clearly stated as such to the workmen on whose attitude to such schemes their success depends. I cannot see that the owners have any right to object to such clear speaking. But they have objected, and the objection has been sustained.

22.   I therefore beg to tender my resignation.

(Signed) FRANCIS JOHNSON,
Industrial Relations Officer.

THE END